Minibus Servic

MINIBUS SERVICES
A Practical Operator's Guide

Paul Fawcett   FCIT MBIM Cert Ed

BOOKS
BOOKS
BOOKS

Croner Publications Ltd
Croner House
London Road
Kingston upon Thames
Surrey KT2 6SR
Tel: 01-547 3333

Copyright © 1989 Paul Fawcett
First published 1989

Published by
Croner Publications Ltd
Croner House
London Road
Kingston upon Thames
Surrey KT2 6SR
Telephone 01-547 3333

While every care has been taken
in the writing and editing of this book,
readers should be aware that only Acts of Parliament
and Statutory Instruments have the force of law,
and that only the courts can authoritatively
interpret the law.

British Library Cataloguing in Publication Data

Fawcett, P. (Paul)
Minibus services: a practical opertor's guide
1. Community minibus services. Organisation – Manuals
I. Title
361

ISBN 1-85452-007-5

Printed in Great Britain by
Ebenezer Baylis & Son Ltd
The Trinity Press, Worcester, and London

Contents

CHAPTER 1 *Background*

Minibus Magic
The Minibus Revolution
Minibuses Shape Up
Minibuses to the Fore
Minibuses Far and Wide

These are just some of the headlines which have appeared in the transport press in the years immediately preceding and following the deregulation of bus services in 1986.

Why the sudden popularity of the minibus? This phenomenon is not simply a by-product of bus deregulation; the minibus revolution began before the Transport Act 1985 was even a Bill. For at least three decades before that senior managers in the bus industry had been telling their "customers" (passengers and the local authorities who were increasingly supporting them financially) that minibuses did not make sound economic sense. Could they all have been wrong?

The minibus phenomenon

This book is a serious attempt to explain the minibus phenomenon of the 1980s and to help bus operators, central and local Government officers, teachers and welfare workers running minibuses and transport students to understand the technical, social, economic and political factors which have contributed to it.

It is a phenomenon. In 1985 the Transport and Road Research Laboratory (TRRL) estimated that there were 63,300 minibuses in operation. The most recent post deregulation figure published is an estimate of 80,000 vehicles made by the National Advisory Unit for Community Transport. As recently as the Spring of 1988, the magazine "Coachmart and Bus Operator", in a supplement devoted to minibuses, estimated that there had been approximately 8000 new minibuses registered by Public Service Vehicle (PSV) operators in the preceding year.

The relative scale of minibus use by different operating sectors, as surveyed by the TRRL, is shown below.

PSV operation	12%
Company personnel carriers	25%
Private ownership	13%

Schools/colleges	18%
Recreational	9%
Community Transport	4%
Statutory – health	
– education	
– social services	17%
Other	2%

It seems reasonable to assume that much of the growth of minibus operations (approximately 17,000 extra vehicles not included in the TRRL figure of 12%) has taken place in the PSV sector, although there has also been a significant growth in Community Transport operations.

Early minibuses

Whilst the minibus will probably earn a place in popular mythology as the passenger carrying vehicle of the 1980s, it has much earlier beginnings. Professor Hibbs, in his book "The Country Bus", points out that many of the small operators of the 1920s established themselves with "light and nippy vehicles", of which the 14 seater Ford Model T was a legend in its own time.

It was in the context of rural bus operation that interest in minibuses resurfaced in the 1960s after the era of high passenger demand. This era had lasted up to and throughout the second world war and well into the post war years but began to wane before the twin onslaught of increasing car and television ownership.

The rural transport panacea?

A committee of inquiry into "Rural Bus Service", the Jack Committee of 1961, looked very carefully at the "small vehicle solution" but concluded that "minibuses are not the universal panacea" and that rural services would need to receive an increasing subsidy from the public purse if they were to be retained.

The Jack Committee concluded that the higher initial capital cost of a large bus could be offset by depreciating it over a longer period than that of a minibus. Neither labour (the most significant operating cost) nor fuel (which would become less significant if, as they recommended, fuel tax rebate were introduced) were low enough, when comparing the operating costs of a minibus to those of a large vehicle, to provide the necessary economics of scale to justify separate minibus fleets. In addition, despite the poor passenger loadings on most rural services, there was often a noticeable schools transport peak which could only be dealt with by a large vehicle.

Two operators in the 1960s did, however, achieve some success with minibuses on rural services, albeit from radically different perspectives. One of these, Mr Chris Taylor, started a minibus service in the Lake District using small vehicles to penetrate narrow valleys and negotiate mountain passes which were inaccessible to conventional buses. Despite opposition from the established large bus operator when he applied for the (then) necessary Road Service Licence in the traffic courts, Mr Taylor succeeded in building up a network of services which quickly became known to tourists and walkers as well as local people.

Much of his success came from his imaginative marketing of the buses as "Mountain Goats", with a black goat silhouette painted on white vehicles which had distinctive roof racks (for rucksacks) reached by a ladder at the rear of the bus.

The brand name Mountain Goat became synonymous with Lake District buses, particularly minibuses. However, the service was seasonal and aimed at the tourist rather than the rural dweller, despite the latter's considerable use of it.

Post Buses

The other successful operator was the Post Office. Mr Trevor Carpenter of the Scottish Postal Board purchased a fleet of Dodge minibuses which he put into service in rural parts of Scotland as Post Buses. The idea of passengers and mail travelling together is as old as the mail coach. The novelty of this service was the way in which the requirement for a vehicle to make two trips per day into deep rural areas, to deliver and then in the afternoon to collect the mail, was used as the basis to "bolt on" a bus service.

The capital costs of a Post Bus, at that time, could be less than those of the van it replaced since the Transport Act 1968 had introduced a 50% bus grant towards the cost of new vehicles which were to be used 50% or more of their time on stage carriage services.

The Post Office never claimed that the service which their buses gave exactly met the travel demands of their passengers. The mail came first and the passengers often had to sit long hours on a vehicle whilst it did its rounds before reaching their destinations. But in areas where there never had been a service or which had recently lost one, the Post Bus was a welcome innovation.

Dial-a-ride

By the end of the 1960s rural transport was not the only problem of the bus industry. In urban areas the familiar vicious circle of increasing car ownership, congestion, slower journey times, falling patronage and increasing fares, which in turn led to a further drop in patronage, more car trips and more congestion, was causing concern to both operators and central and local Government.

In an attempt to tackle this the Transport Act 1968 introduced bus grants (already mentioned) and revenue support. Despite this, the decline continued, especially in those suburbs where car ownership was high. In some cases these became almost as difficult to serve as deep rural areas.

One imaginative solution was dial-a-ride, a "demand responsive" public transport system which employed minibuses on semi fixed routes which could be diverted by radio to pick up and set down passengers at their doors for a premium fare. The concept relied upon there being a high proportion of the population with telephone access in the area chosen for the scheme so that demand could be "adequately expressed".

Well publicised schemes operated in places like Solihull (Birmingham), Sale (Manchester), Carteton (Oxford) and Harrogate, but none of these survive today.

However, the dial-a-ride experiment presaged the minibus revolution in one important way. Operators clearly saw that the success of minibuses would depend not just on retaining what captive traffic there was (children, housewives, pensioners) but in generating new custom.

Community Transport

The welfare minibus taking old folks to their day centre is a familiar sight. What many operators fail to realise is the extent to which their own services are simply inaccessible to many thousands of passengers whose mobility is impaired. In some cases this inaccessibility actually represents a commercial loss of revenue which, in the case of many frail but ambulant passengers, can be regained by redesigning vehicles to make boarding and alighting easier, or by operating specially adapted vehicles on pre-advertised routes and timings.

However, in many more cases the passenger is not even able to reach the bus stop unaided and requires a purpose built vehicle to ride in, possibly with a tail lift and wheelchair restraints. Community Transport schemes, usually operating specially adapted minibuses, are able to cater for this market.

The essence of Community Transport is that whilst it offers a fare paying service to those with impaired mobility, it does not provide a service for "the public at large", nor does it "ply for hire" on fixed routes.

The service is scheduled by "despatchers" who take bookings from the registered clientele of the Community Transport scheme and skilfully match them, sometimes with the aid of sophisticated computer software, to these "many to many" (or taxi type) journeys.

In the past schemes have relied heavily on temporary labour recruited via the Training Agency's now defunct Community Programme. The Employment Training Programme which replaces this is seen by many Community Transport schemes as a less suitable source of staff. Indeed some schemes which are funded by Labour controlled Metropolitan District Councils have been forbidden by their political masters to recruit from this source. In some cases the local Passenger Transport Executive has been persuaded to step in with funds to rescue the scheme.

Community Transport is not a threat to existing public transport operators, whether privately or publicly owned, because the clientele is different. In one sense it is public transport, albeit catering for a narrow and defined sector of the public.

Community Buses

Inevitably, the Community Bus and Community Transport become confused in the minds of some operators and the public.

The Community Bus most emphatically is a minibus. It is a vehicle with between 9 and 16 seats whose operator (often a managing committee of villagers) holds a Community Bus Permit.

This allows them to provide a Community Bus service which carries members of the public at separate fares and also to operate the vehicle for hire and reward at other times where this will financially support the Community Bus service.

It has been remarked that this last provision, preserved in the Transport Act 1985, enshrines a form of cross subsidy in an Act whose purpose was to eliminate the cross subsidising of unremunerative services by "commercial" ones in favour of a form of specific service subsidies won by tendering. The Act does in fact allow the holder of a Community Bus Permit to tender for the subsidised provision of a local service.

Although both types of operation make the vehicle a PSV, the driver, who must be a volunteer (but may be reimbursed his or her expenses and compensated for any loss of earnings), need not hold a PSV driver's licence.

Since a Community Bus service is a local service available to the public at large it must be registered with the Traffic Commissioner like any other local bus service.

Whilst the Community Bus represents in the main a response to the rural transport problem and Community Transport is to be found mainly in urban areas (often inner city areas), there are a few exceptions to this rule. For example, there are one or two Community Buses in urban parts of the Home Counties and a few Community Transport Schemes developing in rural areas. What distinguishes both is their predominant (and in the case of Community Buses, exclusive) use of minibuses.

Car sharing

Technically any passenger vehicle which carries passengers at separate fares for hire and reward is a PSV and to use a vehicle in this way without licensing it as a PSV is an offence. However, the practice of car sharing for social and other purposes has always been widespread.

An attempt to legalise and actively encourage this for journeys to work and those arranged for social and other purposes in connection with the activities of clubs and voluntary associations was made by the Transport Act 1978. It applied to passenger vehicles with eight or less seats.

The Transport Act 1980 consolidated and extended the provisions of the 1978 Act by providing that such car sharing journeys would not be treated as being made in the course of a business of carrying passengers (in other words as a hire and reward PSV operation) if the "fare" or aggregate "fares" did not exceed the runnings costs (including depreciation) of the vehicle for the journey and providing that the arrangements for payment were made before the journey began. Both the above 1978 and 1980 provisions were consolidated into the Public Passenger Vehicles Act 1981.

Another section of the same Act removed the final barrier to car sharing by providing that an insurer could not insert an exclusion clause in a third party insurance policy if this would invalidate the insurance when the vehicle was used under a car sharing agreement.

Car sharing, especially in rural areas, is now widespread. Organisations like the WRVS often organise car pools to make socially desireable transport provisions. Several eight seater vehicles which can carry the maximum number of passengers under a car sharing agreement have come on the market recently, particularly since the Transport Act 1985 which, in making provision for taxis to carry passengers at separate fares, increased the maximum size of a taxi from seven to eight passenger seats. These vehicles resemble small minibuses.

Experiments with minibus services

An initiative tried in 1977 by the Department of Transport allowed local authorities to request the Secretary of State for Transport to designate the whole or part of their area as an experimental area. Within this area the local authority could grant authorisation for the use of passenger vehicles for hire or reward (whether or not at separate fares).

Authorisations could be one of two kinds:
  (a) *general*, applying to any "private" vehicles with 16 or less seats (and these could include minibuses) which would not normally (other than under such an authorisation) be used to carry passengers for hire and reward and,

(b) *specific*, applying either to specific "private" minibuses or to specific "commercial" vehicles which, like taxis, were normally used to carry passengers for hire and reward, and in addition applying to the carriage of specific persons or classes of person.

Some "Shire Counties", such as Devon, made imaginative use of their powers under the PSV (Experimental Areas) Act 1977 and produced schemes for car pools, minibus/taxi/bus/rail co-ordination, rural transport "brokerages" and social and welfare journeys, which were promoted under the banner of the Department of Transport's "Rutex" scheme.

The Act was repealed in 1985 when bus deregulation made its provisions redundant but it did provide "laboratory" conditions under which small scale rural transport minibus operation could be monitored and studied.

Taxi buses

The Department of Transport's White Paper "Buses", which presaged bus deregulation, had this to say about the public transport role of taxis.

> Taxis and Private Hire Cars have become an increasingly important form of passenger transport . . . There will always be bus routes where there are simply not enough travellers to warrant the use of large vehicles. Studies suggest that services might be operated more economically using taxis as buses . . .
>
> The Government proposes to make such services possible by allowing taxis to carry passengers at separate fares . . .

Although this proposal was given effect by the Transport Act 1985, there is scant evidence as yet that the hopes expressed in the White Paper have been realised. A few taxi bus services have been registered in both rural and urban areas. Some of those in rural areas were initiated using the Rural Bus Grant payable under the Act through the Development Commission (in England) and the Scottish and Welsh Offices (in Scotland and Wales respectively).

One large Passenger Transport Executive (PTE) which recently put out a tender for all night taxi buses on Sunday to Thursday nights (when loadings are traditionally low) received no bids.

The Act permitted the carriage of passengers at separate fares by taxis in three different ways. First of all, taxis and private hire cars are now allowed to pick up pre-booked groups of passengers and carry them at separate fares.

Secondly, where the local authority permits it, licensed taxis (but not private hire cars) can pick up passengers who are all travelling in the same direction from designated ranks and charge them separate fares. The consent of the first hirer is required before the driver can accept further fares. In London, ranks at main line stations and Heathrow Airport are already designated for shared taxis. If 10% or more of the licensed taxi operators request it, the local authority must designate ranks for shared taxis. The system is not unlike the "black taxi" system which operates unofficially within the Belfast sectarian areas.

Finally, and of much greater interest to minibus operators, there is provision for a licensed taxi operator to apply to the Traffic Commissioner for a special restricted PSV operator's licence (O licence) to operate a taxi bus. The taxi operator can then register a local service, either as a "commercial service" on which he or she hopes to make a profit (perhaps even in competition with an existing minibus service), or as a service operated under a service subsidy agreement which has been entered into with a local authority after submission of a successful tender.

The vehicle used can have as many as eight passenger seats. The driver need not hold a PSV driver's licence and, when used as a taxi, the vehicle need not be treated as a PSV. This means that the driver, when using the taxi as a bus, is only subject to the domestic drivers' hours regulations (EC drivers' hours regulations do not apply to either minibuses on national journeys or buses on registered local services). He or she could drive the vehicle as a taxi during a rest period!

Nor does the operator, in order to satisfy the Traffic Commissioner as to his or her suitability to hold a restricted PSV O licence, have to be of good repute, professionally competent or of adequate financial standing. The view of the Department of Transport (although not that of most bus operators, who fear unfair competition from taxi buses) is that the process of licensing the vehicle as a taxi with the relevant local authority contains "equivalent but not identical quality controls".

Restricted PSV O licences for minibuses

There are people like hotel proprietors, travel agents, "off airport" long stay car park operators and employers with "personnel carriers" who wish to operate "courtesy" minibuses commercially for their clients or employees.

The Public Passenger Vehicles Act 1981 recognises this type of activity by providing that such operators may obtain a restricted PSV O licence for either a PSV with eight or less seats or for a minibus PSV with sixteen or less seats on national or international operations when used:

(a)   otherwise than in the course of a business of carrying passengers, or

(b)   by a person whose main occupation is not the operation of public service vehicles with nine or more seats.

Unfortunately this last proviso has been exploited by taxi operators to licence minibuses within their fleets, arguing that they are not PSV operators.

The Transport Act 1985 partially closed this loophole by providing that no operator (with the exception of the Post Office with their large Post Bus fleet which is mainly run on restricted licences) could specify more than two minibuses on a restricted licence.

So far the competition between bus operators and taxi operators with restricted licences has been in the field of private hire. A darts team, for example, looks lost in a 52 seater coach but fits neatly into a minibus. Bus operators with minibus fleets are increasingly fighting back against this competition by finding off peak private hire work for their vehicles.

Permit minibuses

Yet another sort of minibus operation which, whilst being non commercial, nevertheless can be construed as the carriage of passengers at separate fares, is the use of minibuses by bodies concerned with:

(a)   education;
(b)   religion;
(c)   social welfare;
(d)   recreation;
(e)   other activities of benefit to the community.

Like care sharing, this type of operation has been carried out unofficially for a long time by schools, scout troops, churches, clubs and other bodies. The distinguishing feature of the operation is that members of the general public are not carried for profit.

The Minibus Act 1977, whose provisions are now to be found consolidated in the Transport Act 1985, legalises such operations. It is this legislation which is used by Community Transport schemes.

Minibus Permits can be issued by the Traffic Commissioner or by designated "eligible bodies", concerned with education, religion, welfare or recreation to bodies who wish to use a minibus in accordance with the Permit's conditions. These are that only the body's own members or clients are carried and the minibus is used "noncommercially" (that is, not with a view to profit).

The driver must be 21 or over and hold a full driver's licence but need not hold a PSV driver's licence and the vehicle must comply with conditions of fitness, which, for new minibuses, are contained in schedules 6 and 7 of the 1986 Construction and Use Regulations.

Traffic Commissioners may also issue Permits for large buses with 17 or more seats, although discussion of these is outside the scope of this book.

How mini is a minibus?

The 1986 Construction and Use Regulations contain a definition of a bus. This is a passenger carrying vehicle adapted to carry more than eight seated passengers in addition to the driver. The regulations go on to define a minibus as having more than eight but not more than sixteen passenger seats. A large bus, according to a later amendment to the regulations, has 17 or more seats.

However, the term minibus, as used loosely by bus operators and the general public, simply means a small bus. In fact, as if further to confuse matters, the Minibus Permit Regulations even define a small bus as having 9–16 seats. (It is not so long ago that the threshold between mini and bus for domestic/EC drivers' hours and tachograph purposes was 14 seats!)

There is no doubt that the original minibus revolution was conceived using small buses, typically Ford Transits, with 16 or less seats. But with revolution has come evolution. Minibuses are more often now 20–24 seat vehicles, either "stretched" versions of the original small bus, or a new breed of purpose built "minis". Technically they are large buses.

Chapter 4 explains how minibus evolution has developed. At this stage it is perhaps worth noting that the development is still proceeding. Manufacturers are producing, and operators are acquiring, vehicles with 30–35 seats.

These vehicles are being described as "midibuses", although there is as yet no use of this term in legislation, which still makes no distinction between any different classes of vehicles with 17 or more seats.

As is now well known, the first serious large scale experiments with urban minibus operation took place in Exeter in 1984. They marked a radical departure from previous experience in so far as minibuses were used to replace conventional buses.

A consequence of the evolution of mini to midi must be that the replacement ratio of $2\frac{1}{2}$ or 3 minis to one conventional bus must inevitably be lowered. This in turn implies a reduction in the frequency of the service.

The problem is that the success of the minibus revolution has been achieved not so much by cost cutting (indeed, overall, operating costs may have risen in some cases), but by the way in which minibuses have captured the imagination of their passengers and actually generated new ridership.

Evidence shows that high frequencies, giving what Mr Anthony Shepherd (the operator who proposed the ill fated London Associated Minibus Operators' Scheme – AMOS) called "PCNW" (perceived continuity, no waiting), are a major marketing ploy. Any visitor to Blackpool, where the slogan "Always a tram in sight" is self evident, can vouch for the success of this strategy.

It is also evident that the small scale of the minibus, creating an immediate intimacy between the passengers and driver, is another major marketing factor. Passengers feel less threatened than, say, on the top deck of a double deck bus, or in a large empty saloon late at night.

Finally, there is what has been described as Mr R Montgomery, the first Manager of Bee Line Minibuses in South Manchester, as the Heineken effect: "Minibuses reach those parts that other buses cannot reach".

Will the midibus do the same, or will it be the victim of its own success?

CHAPTER 2 *Licensing*

In the previous chapter, which briefly traced the history of minibus usage, various types of operation were described. Reference was made to conventional bus operations, carrying the public either at separate fares or as a party, Community Bus operation, educational and welfare Permit operations, Community Transport schemes, "non commercial" operations and taxi bus operations. All of these require licensing in one way or another.

The only kind of minibus operation which is free of any licensing control is the use of a minibus to provide entirely free transport, where there is no element of hire or reward and the vehicle can be taxed as a private light goods vehicle and used as one might use one's own car.

Since technically, as explained below, any vehicle in which passengers are carried for hire and reward is a public service vehicle, a PSV O licence should be held by the operator of the vehicle. Indeed many of the commercial minibus networks are today operated by bus companies who hold such a licence.

However, since an O licence is effectively a quality licence intended to ensure the safe operation of each licensed PSV and because many of the non-commercial uses made of minibuses only technically make them PSVs, legislation ranging from relaxations of standard PSV O licensing (restricted and special restricted licences) to Permit operation of minibuses and Community Buses has developed to facilitate such activities.

The purpose of each of these alternatives has already been explained; this Chapter is intended to describe the process of licensing.

Although outside the scope of this book, it is worth mentioning that bus licensing before deregulation attempted to control the *quantity* of PSV operation by requiring that scheduled bus services were operated under a Road Service Licence. This type of quantity licensing survives today in London (in tandem with the quality provisions of PSV O licensing) as London Local Service Licences. The Secretary of State for Transport has announced his intention of extending deregulation to London.

Holders of such licences, in return for their commitment to providing the service, were granted a virtual operating monopoly on their route. Naturally they guarded this jealously and it was mainly because they tended to perceive the less conventional activities of minibus operators as "abstracting" their traffic and objected to these in the traffic courts that the more relaxed alternative forms of minibus licensing developed.

Quality licences

The Transport Act 1980, most of which was later consolidated into the Public
Passenger Vehicles Act 1981, introduced the concept of a quality licence to control the
safe operation of PSVs. It brought PSV and goods vehicle operation roughly in line
with each other by requiring that the operator, rather than the vehicle, be licensed.

A PSV O licence, naturally enough, is only required if the vehicle is being used
as a PSV. The definition of a PSV is contained in the Public Passenger Vehicles Act
1981 and is quite complex. Nevertheless, it is of fundamental importance for operators
to appreciate when their use of a minibus makes it a PSV and for this reason it is
examined here.

What is a PSV?

Not every bus (ie passenger carrying vehicle with nine or more seats) is necessarily a
PSV, and conversely, a small passenger carrying vehicle with eight or less seats can,
in certain circumstances, be a PSV. It depends on how the vehicle is used. *Any vehicle
with nine or more seats used for hire and reward will be a PSV.*

Hire and reward includes both:
(a)   carriage at separate fares and
(b)   carriage of a party at a composite fare (private hire).

Any vehicle with eight or less passenger seats which carries passengers at separate
fares will also be a PSV. Taxis normally carry at a composite fare, although the
Transport Act 1985 does contain provisions which allow them, under certain circumstances, to carry at separate fares without becoming a PSV.

"Separate fares" covers all payments made by individual passengers, even if they
are not made directly to the driver or operator. For example, an admission ticket for
an event which allows travel on a vehicle to and from that event will be a separate
fare and the operator will require a PSV O licence.

The operation of "private hire" trips at separate fares (where the organiser hires
a coach or bus from an operator on a lump sum basis and then shares the costs amongst
his or her party) is widespread. The Public Passenger Vehicles Act 1981 permits this
by providing that the hire will not be construed as carriage at separate fares if the
following conditions contained in schedule 1 of the Act are met:
(a)   Neither the driver, owner or operator of the vehicle made the arrangements
        for bringing the party together.
(b)   All passengers make substantially the same journey and there are no fare
        differences based on time or distance travelled.

Is it
a motor vehicle
other than a
tramcar? → No →

Yes ↓

Is it
used for hire
or reward → No →

Yes ↓

Is it
adapted to
carry 9 or more
passengers? → No →

Is it
used at
separate
fares? → No →

Yes ↓

Does
Schedule 1
of PPV Act
apply? → Yes →

No ↓

Is it
used in a
private car or van
sharing
scheme → Yes →

No ↓

Is it
a licensed
taxi used under
S.10/S.11 T.Act
1985? → Yes →

No ↓

Is it
a licensed
taxi being used on
a local
service? ← No

Yes ↓   →

It is not a PSV

It is a PSV

It is not a PSV when
used as a taxi

Definition of a PSV
Note: PPV Act = Public Passenger Vehicles Act 1981

(c) The journey has not been previously advertised to the public at large, except by a notice displayed at a place of work, a church or club, or in a journal circulating mainly amongst the relevant employees, worshippers or club members.

Where free transport is provided, for example by a firm's "personnel carrier", the vehicle does not become a PSV. However, a deduction from earnings to cover such "free" transport would make it a PSV.

Some passenger carrying vehicles engaged on activities which would, by strict interpretation of the legal definition, make them a PSV, can be operated without their operator needing to hold a PSV O licence. These include:

(a) Local Education Authorities' school buses (even when, as the Transport Act 1985 now allows, they are also made available to the public at large);

(b) Community Buses and buses and minibuses operated non-commercially by social, welfare, religious, recreational and educational organisations under a Transport Act 1985 "Section 19 Permit".

PSV O licences

There are three main types of PSV O licence. They are issued by the Traffic Commissioner for the area which includes the vehicles' operating centre(s).

Standard national and international: green discs
Standard national: blue discs
Restricted licences: orange discs

In addition Traffic Commissioners may issue interim licences (yellow discs), special restricted licences (for taxi bus operations) and permits (for minibuses and "other Section 19 buses").

PSV O licences are issued to the operator and are not specific to any vehicle; in other words, they do not identify the vehicles which can be used under them. An appropriate number of O licence discs are issued and one must be displayed on a vehicle when it is used on the licence.

Licences specify the number of vehicles "in possession" of the operator and any further number "to be acquired" (the margin). Any vehicle hired in within the margin of the licence must display a disc (this may of course be taken off an out of service vehicle).

Vehicles temporarily hired in for not more than two weeks may display the disc of the operator from whom they are hired. In this case that person (not the hirer) remains the "operator" of the vehicle responsible for its legal use. Holders of restricted licences can not hire large buses with more than 16 seats from standard licence holders.

Standard PSV O licences

Standard licences permit the operation of any size of PSV. Operators have to satisfy the Traffic Commissioner that:

(a) They have sufficient financial resources to run their vehicles safely either by maintaining them or by contracting out the maintenance. If they contract out, they remain responsible for the condition of the vehicles on the road. Sufficient financial resources is not defined in the 1981 Act, but is determined by the Traffic Commissioner, who may hold a public inquiry for that purpose. If the operator requests it, the Commissioner may hold this in camera.

(b) They are of "good repute" (in other words, they have no previous convictions relating to the misuse of a PSV during the last five years). A leaflet obtainable from Traffic Area Offices contains a complete list of relevant convictions. These relate to obvious matters such as drivers' hours and records, as well as the less obvious, such as failure to comply with a Concessionary Fares Participation Notice.

(c) They are professionally competent, or employ a professionally competent transport manager. (The operator or the manager must have a PSV CPC national qualification) and, for a national/international licence, a PSV CPC international qualification.

The professionally competent transport manager need not be a full time employee of the operator but he or she must continuously and effectively manage the operations.

Restricted PSV O licences

Restricted O licences are issued for the use of small passenger carrying vehicles and minibuses. They are often seen as the back door to an O licence since the requirements concerning the operator's professional competence need not be met. However, the Transport Act 1985 has partially closed this door by providing that an operator may have a maximum of two vehicles.

When eventually the operator obtains a CPC he or she can upgrade the restricted licence to a standard licence.

Licences are issued to operators of PSVs with eight or less seats, or for the operation of PSVs with 9–16 seats (excluding the driver's seat) which are used non-commercially.

Non-commercially has a different meaning in this context than in the context of car sharing or Permit operation and means any operation which is not in the course of the business of an operator of PSVs with over eight seats.

The potential for misuse of restricted O licences by taxi firms has already been noted. Restricted operation can be interpreted to include the use of a minibus by a taxi firm whose main business is not PSV operation and taxi operators are the main users of restricted licences. Since they can now, under the taxi sharing provisions of the Transport Act 1985, charge separate fares when using a taxi with eight or less seats it is hard to see why any taxi operator would want to go to the trouble of getting a restricted licence for anything other than a 9–16 seat minibus.

Other operators, such as hotels or travel agencies with one or two courtesy minibuses, might well find having a restricted licence useful. Another main user is the Post Office (which is not limited to a maximum of two Post Buses).

Applications for a PSV O licence

Applications have to be made at least nine weeks in advance of requirement to the Traffic Area Office of the area in which the vehicles' operating centre will be situated. A separate O licence is needed for each Traffic Area in which vehicles have operating centres. The operating centre is the place where the vehicle is normally kept.

Form PSV 421 on which the application is made contains a declaration that the operator will comply with the many regulations concerning the use of the vehicle, in particular those relating to:

(a) drivers' hours and records;
(b) maintenance of the vehicle;
(c) vehicle carrying capacity;
(d) road traffic regulations, including speed limits.

Police and local authorities may make objections to the granting of an O licence on the grounds that the operator does not appear to them to satisfy the requirements as to good repute, financial standing, professional competence or ability to adequately maintain his or her vehicles.

Traffic Commissioners may attach conditions to operators' licences which might include the maximum number and type of vehicles to be specified, the places where these may pick up and set down, and that the operator complies with the Sporting Events (Control of Alcohol) Act 1985.

The Transport Act 1985 also allows Traffic Commissioners to attach what have become known as section 26 and section 111 conditions to deal with cases where it appears to them that an operator has:

(a) run an unregistered local service;
(b) failed to run a registered local service or not run it as registered, or run it in a dangerous manner;
(c) failed to maintain his or her vehicles satisfactorily

or that he or she or an employee or agent has intentionally interfered in the running of another operator's local service.

Commissioners will take account of whether the operator's conduct was reckless or intentional, the frequency of the misconduct and the danger to the public. They may also restrict the vehicles to be used under the licence to specified ones.

Section 26 conditions allow the Traffic Commissioner to prohibit the operator from providing any (or a specified) registered local service and s. 111 enables him or her to reduce by 20% the fuel tax rebate granted to an operator during a three month period if that operator can be shown to have operated a registered local service unreliably or not in accordance with the registered details or to have failed to register the operations.

The Commissioner must also hold a public inquiry before attaching any conditions to the licence unless it seems necessary to do so immediately. Even then, if requested by the licence holder within 28 days, the Traffic Commissioner must still hold an inquiry as soon as it is reasonably practical for him or her to do so.

The Commissioner can also impose traffic regulation conditions on an operator's licence (but only at the request of a Traffic Authority) to regulate, amongst other matters, routes, stopping places and the length of layover time taken by drivers at terminuses. He or she may however only do so to reduce severe congestion or to prevent danger to other road users.

Section 26 and 111 conditions and traffic regulation conditions are very relevant matters for an operator providing urban minibus services under a PSV O licence to consider.

Because operators' licences are quality licences, in effect the passenger's guarantee as to the safety and reliability of the provider of the bus service, Traffic Commissioners are given certain sanctions which they can use against recalcitrant operators.

They may suspend, curtail or revoke a PSV O licence for breaches of the regulations concerning drivers' hours and records, mechanical condition of the vehicle or contravention of any conditions attached to the licence. S. 17 of the Public Passenger Vehicles Act 1981 ensures that if they are requested to do so by an O licence holder they will hold a public inquiry.

Appeals against a Traffic Commissioner's refusal to grant a licence, a suspension, curtailment, revocation or premature termination of the licence, or any condition he or she attaches to it, now have to be made to the Transport Tribunal. The only exception to this rule is that appeals against the imposition of traffic regulation conditions are disposed of by the Secretary of State for Transport.

Since the revocation of an O licence effectively means that the operator can no longer provide a bus service it is sensible to strictly observe the requirements of the Public Passenger Vehicles Act relating to the licence. It may be too late to do anything if a letter arrives from the Traffic Commissioner asking the operator to show him or her "reason why he should not, under s. 17 of the Act, suspend, revoke or curtail the licence".

CHAPTER 3 *Operation*

The two major costs of operating minibuses are incurred in relation to the driver and the vehicle. This chapter examines some of the social, legal and economic factors affecting both of these which operators need to consider.

Drivers

As explained in the last chapter, not every minibus driver needs to hold a PSV driver's licence but, where the minibus is licensed as a PSV and so used, the driver must hold a *vocational* (PSV driver's) licence.

Eurolicences

A proposal by the European Commission that drivers of all passenger vehicles with over eight passenger seats should have to comply with the EC law on driving licences is presently being considered by the Department of Transport.

The Road Traffic (Driver Licensing and Information Systems) Bill 1989 will, when enacted, replace the present dual (ordinary and vocational) licensing system in the United Kingdom with a unified licence issued by the Driver and Vehicle Licensing Centre at Swansea. (Traffic Commissioners presently issue PSV drivers' licences.)

The EC directive on which the Bill is based requires that drivers of passenger vehicles with more than eight seats should hold a "passenger carrying vehicle" licence. No distinction is made between PSVs and non PSVs.

The directive is itself based on a United Nations convention (the Vienna Convention) which provides for a single class of passenger carrying vehicle licence, with a possible further class of licence for articulated vehicles. (The distinction made by the United Kingdom PSV driving licence system between different classes of single-deck vehicles and double-deckers is somewhat redundant now that certain high floor coaches are actually taller than some motorway double-deckers!)

The Department of Transport is seeking from Brussels a derogation (ie exemption for national journeys) from this directive for 9–16 seater vehicles.

PSV drivers' licences

Modern traffic conditions demand especially high standards and skills from those who drive PSVs.

The licensing of PSV drivers is controlled by the Traffic Commissioners. They must be satisfied that drivers who wish to drive PSVs have the necessary skills to carry passengers in safety and comfort and show courtesy and consideration to other road users. To ensure this, first time applicants for PSV drivers' licences are normally required to pass a stringent practical driving test.

Therefore, in addition to holding an ordinary driving licence or a Northern Ireland (ordinary) driving licence which is valid for the vehicle, the driver of a PSV used as a public service vehicle on the road to carry passengers for hire or reward must hold a current PSV driver's licence.

It is an offence for an employer to employ someone to drive a PSV to carry passengers for hire or reward unless that person holds an appropriate ordinary driving licence and a PSV driver's licence.

However, it is sufficient for the driver of a PSV being used other than as a public service vehicle on the road for carrying passengers for hire or reward, eg running empty between depots, staff buses (on which no fare paying passenger is carried), road tests by fitters, etc to hold an ordinary driving licence.

Note also, that this arrangement applies in respect of a vehicle whose use as a PSV has been permanently discontinued, eg a preserved vehicle.

The holder of a PSV driver's licence may drive a rigid goods vehicle not exceeding 10 t unladen weight which is owned by the PSV operator and which is being driven on the operator's behalf to aid or recover a broken down and currently licensed PSV.

Drivers of Community Buses or of school buses owned by a Local Education Authority do not need a PSV driver's licence. Neither do drivers of "Permit" minibuses, as these are not classed as PSVs.

Minimum age limits

The minimum age for a PSV driver is 18 years. Such a driver if so licensed is, however, restricted to:
  (a) driving PSVs on regular services on routes not exceeding 50 km;
  (b) driving passenger vehicles having not more than 17 seats (including the driver) on national transport operations;
  (c) driving "out of service" PSVs.
An out of service PSV may also be driven by an 18 year old:
  (a) when the driver is undergoing a PSV driving test;
  (b) when the driver is supervised by someone who holds a PSV driver's licence.
In other circumstances the minimum age is 21 years.

An out of service PSV which has more than eight passenger seats may be driven by a person who is 21 years old and holds an ordinary driving licence. The minimum age for driving an out of service vehicle with eight or fewer passenger seats is 17 years.

Application for a PSV driver's licence

An application for a PSV driver's licence must be made on form PSV150 and be submitted to the Traffic Commissioner in the area in which the applicant resides. If this is a first application, form PSV447 should also be completed for a PSV driving test appointment. No licence will be granted unless the Commissioner considers the applicant to be a fit person. Evidence may be required that he or she is of appropriate age and can read and write. Additionally, a certificate is required from the applicant's present or last employer and a certificate of character must be produced, signed by two householders or ratepayers who have known the applicant for the past three years.

Medical evidence will be required to the effect that the applicant is not suffering from any disease or physical disability which may prevent him or her undertaking the duties of a PSV driver. In particular, evidence must be submitted that the applicant has not at any time suffered an epileptic attack since attaining the age of five years.

Applicants are required to pass a PSV driving test unless:

(a) the Traffic Commissioner is satisfied that at some time in the preceding five years the applicant held a PSV driver's licence or a Northern Ireland PSV driver's licence for the class of vehicle concerned;

(b) the applicant is a person entering Great Britain from an EC country to take up *permanent residence* who is qualified to drive a PSV by holding a Community licence of the appropriate class in an EC country; has been resident in Great Britain for not more than 18 months and been granted a British ordinary driving licence and can show that at the time of taking up residence he or she had been in the habit of driving a PSV for at least six months in the last 18 months or one year in the last three years;

(c) the application is for a licence restricted to vehicles with eight or fewer seats and the Traffic Commissioner is satisfied as to the applicant's competence.

Cost and duration of PSV drivers' licences

Full	£22.50 for five years
Duplicate or exchange	£5

The PSV driving test

A driving test must be passed before a person can drive a vehicle in public service and in order to do this the applicant must present him or herself together with a suitable vehicle which is in a clean and roadworthy condition and which the examiner accepts as being suitable for the category of licence being sought. (In the Metropolitan traffic area only, the vehicle must be a licensed PSV unless dispensation is granted by the

Traffic Commissioner.) The examiner will test the applicant's competence and in particular will have regard to the following items:

(a) knowledge of the highway code;

(b) knowledge of components relating to safety of the vehicle;

(c) competence to drive the vehicle and in particular that the driver can:

   (i)   start the engine;

   (ii)   move off straight ahead and at an angle;

   (iii)   adopt and keep a safe position in respect of the vehicle in front;

   (iv)   overtake safely;

   (v)   turn right and left;

   (vi)   make an emergency stop, safely;

   (vii)   stop under normal conditions;

   (viii) reverse into a restricted opening to the right or to the left and stop the vehicle in a predetermined position;

   (ix)   give appropriate signals;

   (x)   respond and react to traffic signs and signals.

The PSV driving test is now similar in most respects to the HGV driving test in that both are of the same duration ($1\frac{1}{2}$ hours) and conducted partly on the public road and partly off it (to test manoeuvring skills).

The PSV test may be conducted by a Department of Transport examiner, or an authorised examiner working for an operator with a large number of PSVs.

A dual (PSV and ordinary driving licence) test may be conducted for the holder of a provisional driving licence.

Trainees

Trainees driving PSVs under a provisional licence must be accompanied by a fully qualified licence holder. The vehicle must display "L" plates at the front and rear.

Test fee

The fee for a PSV driving test is £42. If a test is cancelled for a reason beyond the driver's control and no alternative appointment can be made the fee is refunded. If the driver cancels the test a refund may be given only if three clear days' notice is given (this excludes the day on which notification is received, Saturdays, Sundays and Bank Holidays).

PSV licence and badge

A successful applicant will be issued with a PSV licence and badge, which is valid for five years in all traffic areas. The licence must be signed by the holder and the PSV driver's badge must be worn in a conspicuous place when on duty, so that the distinguishing letters and numbers are easily legible.

A change of address must be notified to the Commissioner within seven days.

A PSV licence must be produced on demand to a police officer, certifying officer, or PSV examiner, or, in default, the driver must produce it within seven days (when required by a police officer) or within 10 days in other circumstances.

If a PSV licence or badge is lost or destroyed or becomes defaced or illegible, the facts must be reported to the Commissioner who may issue a duplicate licence or substitute badge.

A fee is payable as a deposit for the issue of a badge, which remains the property of the Commissioner. This fee is refundable when a badge is returned.

Renewals

Renewal of a PSV driver's licence is made by completing form PSV105R. A medical certificate is required for drivers still driving a PSV at the age of 46 years and at each subsequent renewal.

Suspension, revocation and disqualification

If, in the opinion of the Commissioners, the holder of a PSV licence ceases to be a fit person through reason of conduct or physical disability, the licence may be suspended or revoked. In such circumstances the licence and badge must be surrendered within 14 days.

If the holder is disqualified from driving the ordinary licence is lost, which means that he or she is not allowed to drive *any* type of vehicle for as long as the disqualification is in force and the PSV licence is invalid during this period. It does not matter what type of vehicle was being driven at the time the offence was committed.

In such circumstances the holder of a PSV licence and badge must surrender them to the Commissioner in whose area he or she resides within seven days from the date of disqualification. Application for the return of the licence can be made when the ordinary driving licence is restored but the Commissioner has powers to require the applicant to take a PSV driving test before a new licence is issued.

Appeals

If an applicant for, or holder of, a PSV licence is aggrieved by the Commissioner's refusal to grant a licence or failure to lift a suspension, etc on a licence, the aggrieved person may give notice in writing requiring the Commissioner to reconsider the decision. In those circumstances the applicant is entitled to be heard personally or someone may represent him or her.

Anyone who is aggrieved or dissatisfied with the Commissioner's decision on reconsideration, may appeal:

(a) to a Magistrate's Court in England and Wales;

(b) to the Sheriff's Court in Scotland

whose decision is binding on the Commissioner. An existing PSV licence remains in force until the appeal is dealt with.

Classes of PSV licence

The classes of vehicle covered by the PSV licence are as follows.

Category	Type of Vehicle
1	A double-decked vehicle without automatic transmission
1A	A double-decked vehicle with automatic transmission
2	A single-decked vehicle without automatic transmission or a half-decked vehicle without automatic transmission being in either case a vehicle the overall length of which exceeds 8.5 m
2A	A single-decked vehicle with automatic transmission or a half-decked vehicle with automatic transmission being in either case a vehicle the overall length of which exceeds 8.5 m
3	A single-decked vehicle without automatic transmission or a half-decked vehicle without automatic transmission being in either case a vehicle the overall length of which does not exceed 8.5 m but which does exceed 5.5 m
3A	A single-decked vehicle with automatic transmission or a half-decked vehicle with automatic transmission being in either case a vehicle the overall length of which does not exceed 8.5 m but which does exceed 5.5 m
4	A single-decked vehicle without automatic transmission or a half-decked vehicle without automatic transmission being in either case a vehicle the overall length of which does not exceed 5.5 m

4A	A single-decked vehicle with automatic transmission or a half-decked vehicle with automatic transmission being in either case a vehicle the overall length of which does not exceed 5.5 m
5	A vehicle specified in item 4 and 4A above but restricted to uses specified in the licence

Types of vehicle which may be driven by holders of various PSV licences are given below.

Class of vehicle specified in licence	Other vehicles which may be driven
1	1A, 2, 2A, 3, 3A, 4 and 4A
1A	2A, 3A and 4A
2	2A, 3, 3A, 4 and 4A
2A	3A and 4A
3	3A, 4 and 4A
3A	4A
4	4A
4A	None
4B	None

Automatic transmission includes in practice semi-automatic, pre-selector and vario-matic transmission.

A driver may not drive a PSV above the categories for which he or she is licensed. A driver whose licence is endorsed for a vehicle fitted with automatic transmission is restricted to that type of vehicle.

Preparation for the test

Applicants should study:
(a) the Highway Code;
(b) DTp Pamphlets DL68 "Your Driving Test";
(c) DLP68 "PSV Drivers' Licences";
(d) "Driving" – the DTp manual from HMSO and most bookshops.
They should also make sure they know the rules regarding:
(a) equipment which must by law be carried on a PSV;

(b) conduct of drivers and passengers;

(c) drivers' hours and records regulations;

(d) drivers' responsibilities after an accident.

Applicants should also have a working knowledge of the construction and main component parts of the vehicle, its weight, height, width and length. They should make sure it is roadworthy, has sufficient fuel for the test, displays L plates front and rear (for a dual test) has a road tax disc and a secure seat for the examiner. Applicants must bring their ordinary provisional licences with them and be punctual.

Working knowledge of the vehicle is an EC requirement which is now a formal part of the test (it has always been tested informally). Applicants are required to understand enough to appreciate when it is unsafe to drive, to be alert to possible defects and to be able to report verbally or in writing to a fitter or mechanic the repairs thought to be needed.

Offences

A person who drives a public service vehicle on the road without being in possession of the appropriate licence commits an offence. Also an employer who employs a person for this purpose can be prosecuted. In both cases a fine of up to £500 on summary conviction can be imposed.

The driver–salesman concept

Recruitment of minibus drivers has been brisk during the last half decade. In some cases operators setting up brand new minibus networks, especially post deregulation, have needed to employ large numbers of drivers within a short time in order to be able to start up a service quickly ahead of their competitors.

The 42 days' notice of commencement of a service which the regulations covering the registration of local services prescribe has in extreme cases been all the time allowed within which to recruit, select and train new drivers.

Sometimes this exercise has taken place against the backdrop of conventional bus depot closures and a labour market awash with redundant PSV drivers and yet very few of these have actually either wanted or secured the minibus driver posts.

To understand why this has occurred it is necessary to examine two separate but related issues:

(a) the job description of a minibus driver and

(b) minibus drivers' wages.

Customer care

Urban minibus schemes have generally been launched amidst immense publicity. This publicity frequently emphasises the user friendly nature of the service. Features such as "hail and ride" operation are marketed in such a way as to convey the impression of friendly drivers concerned about customer care.

Unfortunately the public perception of some drivers of large buses is often the antithesis of this. The pressures of one person operation of large vehicles in heavy traffic militate against good customer care, and despite the fact that a majority of PSV drivers are considerate of their passengers' needs, a minority develop behaviour patterns which alienate their customers. To a regrettable extent this minority have distorted the general view of drivers.

Operators of minibus services have frequently responded to this situation by expressing a prejudice against employing ex bus drivers to drive their minibuses. A common expression of this thinking has come across in press quotations from minibus operators like "I want salesmen, not drivers".

Despite the use of the term salesmen, a much higher proportion of women have been recruited as minibus drivers than was the case with conventional bus drivers. This is partly because of the perceived easier handling characteristics of minibuses. The fact that some of these women minibus drivers are already driving large buses in the undertakings which recruited them shows this to be a false assumption. There is little doubt also that many managers clearly perceive women as excellent carers and salespersons.

Some ex bus drivers have remarked to the author that since the early minibuses resembled "bread vans" they were not surprised to see them being driven by "bread roundsmen".

Behind the prejudice and the acrimony lies the simple fact that intensive urban minibus operation is market led as opposed to the largely product led pre deregulated bus industry. To succeed, operators need to do more than abstract or capture their competitors' traffic; they also need to generate new traffic which was not present on the conventional services which they aim to replace.

To do this their drivers need to be trained in customer care; to be able to understand the passengers and their needs, fears and problems and to be able to assist them. The drivers need to inspire confidence in the passengers that they will get a smooth and safe ride, and that they will be under good care and surveillence throughout the entire journey. To a large extent they are expected to provide the assurance which passengers lost when conductors were phased out. Hence the operators' reluctance, unfairly perhaps, to employ ex bus drivers.

This reluctance has even persisted where operators have met with enormous delays in the PSV driver testing system because of the large number of new recruits without vocational licences. In the early days of the minibus boom years, especially immediately after deregulation, the DTp's examiners' resources were severely stretched and in parts of the country tests were subject to long delays. Even in these circumstances few operators resorted to the quick route of recruiting ex bus drivers.

Looked at from the ex bus drivers' point of view, there are several reasons why many of them have not even attempted to obtain minibus positions.

In some cases it may simply be that turning to driving a small vehicle, after the "macho image" of a large bus, is perceived as a demotion. In other cases, the generous redundancy agreements reached in the run up to deregulation have left the older drivers who accepted these, and whose family and mortgage commitments are less onerous than those of younger drivers, reasonably well off.

Wages

In most cases the reason lies simply in differences between the wages and conditions of minibus drivers and conventional drivers. The driver who said that he did not want to be a "mini driver on mini wages" probably accurately summed up the feelings of many of his workmates.

A study of the National Bus Company's urban minibus networks in 1987 by Turner and White for the Transport and Road Research Laboratory concluded that "minibus conversions [from conventional bus networks] often result in extended hours of operation. This has been partly possible due to more flexible working arrangements and lower overtime, evening and weekend wage rates".

The introduction of minibuses has been seen by many operators as a chance to negotiate new pay and conditions agreements and to recruit new staff outside the old agreements. Although nationally the Transport and General Workers Union is opposed to separate minibus agreements branches at local level are increasingly accepting these as a hedge against redundancy.

Hourly pay deals allow operators to match vehicles and traffic more closely and facilitate the recruitment of part time staff to cover peaks and other unsociable hours. Productivity agreements can be negotiated doing away with such practices as standard running times in favour of differential peak/off peak running times and resulting in higher average speeds which in turn can result in higher operating frequencies without the need to increase fleet size. (Increases in operating speeds from 11–12 mph to approximately 16 mph are quite common.)

Minibus drivers can take home the same pay as conventional one person operation drivers but they generally earn this from higher productivity and by shedding old restrictive practices.

One problem which has already arisen for large operators making piecemeal conversions from conventional services to minibus operations is the way in which this creates a two tier workforce. This is not only divisive but also reduces operational flexibility in so far as it can prove impossible within existing agreements to switch drivers between services to maximise the productivity of the workforce (or platform staff as they are still referred to by many busmen: a leftover from the days of conductors!).

This problem has been tackled by one large ex PTE bus company by offering its platform staff a generous lump sum incentive to accept a single status remuneration package. This not only consolidated the old pre deregulation pay agreement with its myriad premium payments into a weekly "salary" in return for a flexible roster averaging a standard working week but also telescoped the minibus and one person operation (OPO) rates at an average figure.

Of course not all staff took the incentive and the company still has a two tier salary structure, but sufficient numbers accepted the new scales to enable more flexible working practices to be introduced. Since new staff are recruited on the terms of the single tier agreement, eventually, by a process of natural wastage, the company's entire platform staff will be available for minibus, OPO and even (since this is a relatively new trend in post deregulation competition) conductor operated services.

A further spin off of minibus conversions is that for the first time since the general demise of the conductor there is once more a career path for young entrants to the industry, who can commence driving minibuses at the age of 18 years. The old career path of conductor, driver, inspector may be replaced by a new progression of minibus driver, OPO driver and inspector.

The tyranny of the insurance companies, who in some cases would not look at "big bus" drivers below the age of 25 and thus made the industry a "second chance" employer, is being broken by minibus schemes.

Before leaving the subject of staff, mention should be made of the role of escorts. They carry out an essential function on Community Transport services, helping those whose mobility is impaired to board and alight and in some cases even collecting them from and delivering them to their own front doors.

It is this high degree of customer care which conventional services, even minibuses running to tight schedules, cannot provide and which has encouraged many handicapped passengers to venture once more onto public transport (albeit a dedicated form).

Vehicles

The next chapter looks in considerable detail at the variety of minibuses available, their designs and their limitations. This chapter examines the operational characteristics of the minibus.

Minibuses have the ability to penetrate into areas which it would be difficult, if not impossible to serve using conventional buses. Residential estates with narrow roads and widespread on street parking are now accessible to public transport. The minibus can go to the passenger, rather than the passenger having to go to the bus.

It is also possible to penetrate pedestrianised shopping precincts and new industrial estates, again making minibus services much more accessible than the conventional main road bound bus which they are replacing.

The problem for the operators is that although they can now spread their services much more evenly over an area their resources are inevitably less concentrated. This can be alleviated by "fantailing out" at the suburban trip ends to give a wide choice of destinations but concentrating groups of services along main road corridors and at town centre departure points.

Typically services have little or no layover time at the town centre, simply delivering incoming passengers at a stand as near as possible to their desired destination and collecting a fresh outward load. Layover and recovery periods are usually taken at the outer terminus, which is often a point on a "loop" performed around a housing estate situated off the main corridor.

Since the essence of urban minibus operation is to provide a more frequent service than the conventional bus and in doing so to generate additional traffic, this pattern of service meets these aims. Some operators vary the pattern by either providing cross town services, or by linking two urban centres so that the "thin ends" of the service become in effect a more lightly loaded middle section.

It is even possible for such services to run across each of the two towns to loop terminuses at the other extremity of the built up areas. However, a disadvantage of such a service is the delays caused by congestion which can be twice as bad as on a route serving just one major town centre.

The Transport and Road Research Laboratory Report on NBC urban minibuses referred to earlier found that minibus conversions tended to eliminate cross town services. The conventional wisdom seems to be that high frequency minibus routes should not be much more than five miles in length. Anything greater than that distance is better served by more comfortable conventional buses.

Much has been written about the "replacement" ratio of minibuses to conventional vehicles. The TRRL study found that this was typically 3:1, varying between 3.5:1 and 2.5:1. However, what these figures disguise is the capacity *replacement* ratio. In other words there is all the difference in the world between three full 16 seater minibuses replacing one full 52 seater single-deck bus and three full minibuses replacing one two-thirds empty double-deck bus. At best a simple ratio only indicates the extent to which the frequency of the service has been stepped up.

Schedules

The more frequent the service the more attractive it becomes to passengers and potential passengers. Given that urban minibus schemes, even allowing for the lower capital cost of the buses, the lower wages of the drivers (see Chapter 6) and the faster running times are inherently more expensive than the conventional buses which they replace, their success or failure depends upon their ability to generate new traffic.

The extent to which they are able to do this depends on many factors but frequency of operation and "headway" between vehicles is a paramount consideration. It has been estimated that conventional urban bus services with headways as low as every ten minutes can be vulnerable to high frequency minibus competition.

Ironically, the success of some schemes contains the seeds of their own destruction, in so far as the necessary replacement of minibuses by midibuses has tempted schedulers to reduce frequencies at "slack" times (often the very times where some modest traffic generation has occurred). It has also been argued that a midibus may be inherently less user friendly than a minibus.

Running speeds of minibuses are usually better than those of conventional buses. They are generally more manoeuvrable, can accelerate faster and are able to "nip into" traffic streams more easily than large buses. Boarding and alighting times tend to be less if only because the capacity of the vehicle is less. Leaving passengers at queues where there is another minibus behind is not too serious.

New technology

The TRRL report also commented that radio control of minibuses has been an effective traffic management device in mitigating against the reduction in running speeds due to congestion. It can also be used effectively to maintain even headways so that the passengers perceive a continuity of service.

The use of electronic ticketing machines is widespread on urban minibuses. Not only are drivers saved the tedium and delay of completing waybills at the end of each trip but the machine is able to store complete information relating to every class of passenger (child, OAP, season ticket, dog, etc), boarding and alighting steps, journeys made and vehicle loadings by time, route and location.

This is invaluable for two purposes. It is a powerful marketing tool, enabling the operator to be more demand responsive and is a means of protecting the operators' revenue against dishonest staff and passengers.

Some radio control schemes, especially those utilising the new band three frequencies, convey details from the ticket machine over their carrier waves, so that the controller can "follow" the bus, identify the stage last passed and check the tickets sold on a visual display unit. It is even possible to enable vehicle performance indicators, like engine temperature and oil pressure, to be displayed.

Off-peak services

Some operators are experimenting with alternative uses of those minibuses which would otherwise be garaged at off-peak times, such as evenings and Sundays.

The most obvious of these is private hire work and there is no doubt that the presence of a new fleet of minibuses on the roads prompts many unsolicited private hire enquiries.

The other use, which was probably not predicted, is the substitution of minibuses for conventional buses on routes which are only busy enough during the day to warrant large bus operation. Whilst it never makes sense to have duplicate peak (large bus)/off-peak (minibus) fleets, where there are both types of bus in the garage at night it does make sense to use the least expensive resource if this can adequately do the job.

CHAPTER 4 *Safety*

The safety of passenger carrying vehicles, irrespective of their size or whether they are used as public service vehicles, is a heavy responsibility which the law, quite properly, places on their operators.

The Public Passenger Vehicles Act 1981, by defining the operator of a passenger vehicle as the driver or the person who employs the driver, ensures that ultimately the duty of providing a safe vehicle, driven safely, rests solely with the operator and not with any other parties who might be involved in some way in the operation (such as vehicle suppliers, hirers, leasing companies, bodybuilders, repairers and maintainers).

Of course just as passengers are entitled to assume that the vehicle in which they are carried is fit for the purpose and will ensure that they arrive safely at their destination, so operators must assume that vehicles which they buy from a reputable dealer meet all the legislative requirements for safe operation.

In the final analysis, therefore, it is the responsibility of operators to make clear to suppliers and, if they are not intending to do their own maintenance, the person to whom they contract this, their overriding requirement that all relevant legislation, in respect of the vehicle's initial specification and its subsequent condition, is complied with at all times.

There are sound legal, moral and economic reasons for good maintenance. This should amount to more than just carrying out the manufacturer's recommended servicing. The vehicle should be thoroughly inspected by a competent mechanic at regular intervals of time or mileage (or both).

Any defects should be rectified before the vehicle is put back into service. Drivers should be instructed to complete defect reports (including "nil defect" reports to show that they have examined their vehicles) and these too should be acted upon immediately. Records of inspections, rectifications and maintenance should be kept for at least 15 months, as they may be required by Department of Transport inspectors.

The police have always been able to stop and inspect any motor vehicle on the road, but the Transport Act 1985 has now given Department of Transport vehicle examiners powers to carry out roadside checks (but not random fleet inspections at operators' premises) on minibuses. They may prohibit the use of an unsafe vehicle by issuing a prohibition notice (PG9). Police and vehicle examiners may, however, still inspect any vehicle on any premises where they have the consent of the owner of the premises or the vehicle if they give 48 hours' notice. The notice is not necessary if a vehicle has been reported as having been involved in an accident.

Police may also stop and inspect any motor vehicle on a road, although there is a limited provision for the driver to elect for a deferred test where these wider powers are used.

Operators have a duty to check and satisfy themselves that the law is not being infringed. The purpose of this chapter, therefore, is to say sufficient about the design and construction of minibuses, their equipment and use, and the responsibility for maintaining them to a high standard of fitness, to enable operators who might initially know very little about the "nuts and bolts" of the job, to confidently discharge this onerous duty.

It is not a section by section analysis of the details of the legislation (for which readers are referred to "Croner's Coach and Bus Operations", updated quarterly) but rather an overview of the more important requirements with which operators should familiarise themselves and which they should endeavour to meet.

Vehicle design

Passenger vehicles with nine or more passenger seats are all, according to their definition (to be found in the Construction and Use Regulations), buses. If a bus has between 9 and 16 passenger seats it is, by its legal definition, a minibus.

However, the term minibus, both within the passenger transport industry and as used by the general public, has come to embrace all small passenger vehicles, even where these have more than 16 seats. In describing what is available on the vehicle market the term will be used in its widest sense to mean all small buses.

A new word, midibus, is being coined by the industry to describe passenger vehicles smaller than conventional 45–52 seater single-deck vehicles but larger than minibuses. How large a "mini" has to be before it becomes a "midi" is a matter of conjecture; there is no legal guidance and in fact the word midibus does not appear anywhere in legislation.

We might find a clue to where this threshold will lie in the future if we examine the current marketing strategy of Leyland-DAF, the United Kingdom's leading bus manufacturer. A view often expressed in the mid 1980s by Adrian Wickens, their Market Planning Manager, was that the minibus market was saturated by van derived passenger vehicles leaving little room for further competition, but that minibus operation was proving so successful that eventually operators would inevitably require a larger "midi" bus. To this end they launched their Leyland Swift chassis in 1988, capable of accepting a body with, typically, between 30 and 40 seats. About the same time Hestair-Dennis, another United Kingdom conventional bus manufacturer, produced the Javelin, a 4 m wheelbase chassis for 35 seat bodies. Any vehicle with more than about 30 seats is described in this book as a midibus.

By 1988 Mr Wicken's view was being seriously challenged by at least three vehicle manufacturers who introduced purpose built minibuses to confront the van derived "bread van with seats and windows" image and to try and give operators a vehicle built to "big bus standards". Nevertheless, many substantive operators still appear to prefer van derived vehicles for various technical reasons.

In one respect, however, the view that minibuses would continue to grow in size proved correct, even though they did not, by and large, become midis overnight. By 1988 minibuses were almost unrecognisable alongside their van derived counterparts of the mid 1980s. Typically they were more likely to be of 22 to 27 seat capacity than the earlier 16 seat accomodation and to offer a higher standard of comfort. Often carpeted and with better seat upholstery, they had larger engines and better transmissions to give their passengers a much smoother and quieter ride.

Integral and purpose built minibuses

All of these, the MCW Metrorider, the Peugeot Talbot Pullman and the newer CVE Omni are of integral construction. In other words they do not have a separate chassis and the vehicles' body panels, roof and floor pan are strengthened to do the work of a chassis.

The Omni is a low floor Austrian designed Steyr 23 seater minibus employing a turbocharged Land Rover diesel engine. City Vehicle Engineering claim in their advertisements that the vehicle is built around a safety cage which will give it the sort of crush proof roll over protection now demanded by the EC of all new *coaches* (a much narrower definition than bus). The exceptionally low floor height of the passenger saloon is achieved by replacing the conventional back axle by two self levelling air suspension stub axles at either side of the vehicle. These hardly intrude into its floor pan and can be "let down" to drop the rear entrance almost to road level to accept a wheelchair. The driver's cab, however, is perched well above the passengers, over the engine and front wheel drive.

The Peugeot Talbot Pullman is a purpose built minibus having an integral bus shell on a novel three axle chassis. The rear tandem axle is claimed to give an exceptionally smooth ride and because the drive is to the front wheels the manufacturers have been able to keep the height of the entrance step down to a mere 10 inches.

The Metrorider trys to overcome the perennial moan of minibus passengers that the narrow bodies are designed for mini passengers, by making a wide bodied version available which can take standard big bus seats. There is also a "stretched" 33 seater midibus version.

Van conversions

The remainder of the minibus vehicle market is dominated by the major United Kingdom made and imported van chassis. Prominent amongst these are the products of Fiat, Ford, Freight Rover, Mercedes, Renault/Dodge, Toyota and Volkswagen/MAN. In 1987 Freight Rover supplied in excess of 800 chassis for minibuses, with Dodge supplying just under that amount and Mercedes and Ford each providing between 350–400 chassis.

In the Autumn 1988 Minibus Supplement, "Coachmart and Bus Operator" lists no fewer than 33 converter/coachbuilders who will turn these chassis into minibuses. Some of these specialise in small market niches, such as welfare vehicles, but others are fast becoming well known names in the industry.

Van to minibus conversions like those of Mellor Coachwork, Dormobile, Robin Hood, Walter Alexande, Devon Conversions and Williams are sufficiently familiar sights on our roads to be recognised and logged by bus spotters, whilst some, like the Optare City Pacer, the Crystal Servicebus, the Carlyle Iveco Daily, the Reeve Burgess Beaver and the PMT Bursley are becoming common sights in different locations. The Carlyle and PMT minibuses are manufactured by the bus engineering arms of ex National Bus Company subsidiaries. Since NBC has been credited in a large part with initiating the minibus boom, this is not surprising.

As well as using the all steel integral structure of a complete van body-shell, some converters create coachbuilt bodies on chassis cowls (ie a vehicle chassis complete with driver's cab) supplied for this purpose by the manufacturers. This opens the way to a more versatile form of construction, often allowing wider bodies than can be achieved by using the integral factory shells. Accomodating four seats across the body, instead of the more usual minibus configuration of 2 + 1 seats per row, has enabled Reeve Burgess, using a Mercedes 609D "Dusseldorf Van" chassis cowl and their own bodywork, to gain an extra 6 seats thus uprating their 19 seater Beaver minibus to 25 seats.

An article in the August 1988 issue of "Transport", the magazine of the Chartered Institute of Transport, listed MCW, Carlyle, Alexande, Dormobile and Robin Hood as "amongst the market leaders", and the Freight Rover Sherpa and Dodge as the two most popular chassis for PSV minibuses. The Ford Transit is an equally popular chassis within the wider minibus market of public service, welfare and educational vehicles. The author of the article also estimated that the number of minibuses engaged in PSV operation had increased from just under 2500 in 1986 to approximately 5600 serving some 400 locations by 1988.

Other strong contenders for the midibus market were also identified in the article. These included the PMT Knype built on either the Leyland-DAF Swift chassis or the Mercedes 814 chassis and the Optare Star Rider, a bus which offers accomodation for

33 seated and 8 standing passengers and is also based on the Mercedes. Reeves Burgess too have designed a successful midibus, the coach bodied 33 seater Beaver which uses an extended Mercedes 811D chassis cowl.

Vehicle fitness legislation

Many manufacturers claim that their products comply with schedule 6. This is a reference to a schedule in the Road Vehicles (Construction and Use) Regulations 1986 which prescribes construction requirements for minibuses with 9–16 seats first used on or after 1.4.88. Minibuses manufactured and used before then have the option of complying with schedule 6 or the earlier Minibus (Conditions of Fitness, Equipment and Use) Regulations 1977.

A point seemingly missed by manufacturers who advertise their vehicles as complying with schedule 6 is that the schedule is not applicable to large buses with 17 or more passenger seats. Both PSVs and large buses operated under a Minibus and Other Section 19 Permit Buses Regulations 1987 "red" permit must comply with the full PSV fitness regulations contained in the PSV (Conditions of Fitness, Equipment Certification and Use) Regulations 1981. These latter regulations are much more demanding than schedule 6 and contain requirements relating to the comfort as well as the safety of passengers (for example, minimum seat spacing and leg room are prescribed). It would be inappropriate to include them in a book about minibuses. Readers operating large buses can find details of these 1981 fitness regulations in "Coach and Bus Operations" (Croner), or summarised in "Croner's Coach and Bus Driver's Handbook".

Schedule 6, construction of minibuses

The provisions of schedule 6 are given below. Operators of minibuses registered on or after 1.4.88 must comply with these and operators of older minibuses may comply with them, or with the earlier 1977 regulations. Indeed it is quite likely they would have been constructed to comply with them. Thus a choice as to whether an older minibus should comply with the 1977 or 1986 regulations must be made; it is not permitted to comply partly with the 1977 regulations and partly with the 1986 ones.

Doors

Every minibus must have one service door on the nearside plus an emergency door at the rear or on the offside. (An offside driver's door does not constitute an emergency door but a rear opening service door can do so. Normally, doors with passenger lifts will be designated as service doors, not emergency doors, as they are obviously intended for general use.)

Every emergency door must be clearly marked in letters at least 25 mm in height on both the inside and the outside with the words "EMERGENCY DOOR" or "FOR EMERGENCY USE ONLY", and the means of operation must be clearly indicated on or near the door. It must open outwards and be capable of being manually operated.

When fully opened the emergency door must provide an aperture not less than 1210 mm high and 530 mm wide. Where double doors at the rear are designated as the emergency exit it is the space revealed by the door which opens first which counts, unless both doors are released by a single action.

Any power operated doors must have transparent panels enabling a person immediately outside the door to be seen and such a door must be capable of being operated by the driver from the driving seat. It must also be possible to open the door from both inside and outside the vehicle by the use of overriding controls (clearly marked so as to indicate the means of operation) on or near the door. The marking must state that these controls can be used by passengers *only* in an emergency.

Power operated doors must have sensitive soft edges which will detect trapped limbs and baggage and reverse the closing motion of the door. If such an auto-release system is worked from stored energy it must be designed so as not to adversely affect the operation of the vehicle's brakes.

It must be possible to operate every door from inside the minibus, even if they can be locked from outside. Handles which open doors from the inside must operate with a single movement. This means that if there are separate catches at the top and bottom of the door, these are only acceptable if they can be operated simultaneously by being mechanically linked using a pull cord, metal rods or similar device.

Each door must also be designed, so far as is reasonably possible, with a device capable of holding it closed to prevent passengers falling out of the vehicle. Doors must be hinged at the edge nearest the front of the vehicle and either be closed by a two stage slam lock or protected by a tell tale device which will warn the driver if the door is opened.

The driver must also, by the use of mirrors or otherwise, be able to clearly see the areas both inside and outside every service door. Although this requirement does not extend to emergency doors it is quite strict and provides that in the case of a rear door a person 1.3 m tall (effectively a child) standing 1 m behind the vehicle must be visible to the driver when he or she is seated at the controls of the vehicle. The fitting of a rearscope reversing lens in a rear door window, giving a wide angle view of the road behind, is a common solution to this problem.

There must be unobstructed (except by tilting/folding seats or ramps) access from every passenger seat to at least two doors and a grab handle or hand rail at every side service door to assist passenger boarding or alighting.

For there to be "unobstructed access" where a tail lift is fitted, this must fold down either level with the floor or underneath the vehicle and, where a tip up attendant's seat is fitted at a door (it must *never* be fitted on the door), its mechanism must be readily available to both boarding and alighting passengers. It is doubtful if a folding front seat giving access from the rear of the vehicle to the front nearside door, where there is not a second side door, could fully comply with this regulation. Often the releasing mechanism is hard to get at and the seat is awkward to tip because of the intrusion of seat belts and their anchorages into the "gap" thus created.

A common sense approach to evaluating the extent to which the spirit, if not the letter, of this regulation is met, is to try leaving the vehicle in a hurry to see how easy this is in practice. For example, check that door handles are not obscured by lifts or folded seats and that once these are turned it is possible to push the door(s) open, if necessary arranging that this simultaneously knocks out the lift as well. In the case of a pair of rear doors both should be held shut by the first door and thus be controlled by a single door handle. It is not permissible for the second door to require separate unfastening. It is salutary to recall that it only takes 90 seconds for a minibus to become completely ablaze.

Seats

There are no minimum spacing or leg room requirements for minibus seats but there is a minimum permitted seat width of 400 mm. This measurement can be used to define how many seats there are in vehicles with continuous bench seating. No seat may be fitted to a door. Seats must be properly anchored to the minibus.

Any sideways facing seats situated immediately forward of a rear door must have an armrest or similar device to prevent the occupant falling through the doorway and any seat situated where the occupant could be thrown through any doorway provided with power operated doors or thrown down any steps (including a single step-well) must be fitted with a screen or guard which affords adequate protection against such an occurrence.

Electrical connections

If the electrical circuit is over 100 volts then it must be protected by a dual pole switch accessible to the driver from inside the vehicle. This switch must not extinguish any of the vehicle's obligatory lamps.

There are also sensible prohibitions of electrical circuits carrying a higher current than they are designed for, being inadequately insulated, or not connected via a fuse. (The latter prohibition excludes starter and ignition circuits.)

Often welfare vehicles which are van conversions have so much ancilliary equipment (tail lifts, reversing bleepers, extra lighting, etc) that there is a danger of the original wiring being overloaded. Sometimes the negative earth lead from the battery is unable to cope with the load, a common cause of engine fires. Although circuits exceeding 100 volts are rare, it is still worthwhile considering a dual pole isolation switch as a safety measure.

Fuel tanks, exhaust fumes and other risks to occupants

No fuel tank must be located within the passenger compartment. Exhaust pipe outlets can only be at the rear or offside of the minibus. Conversions of foreign left hand drive van shells or chassis, where the exhaust would normally be on the nearside, will thus require modification.

Regulation 44 of the Road Vehicles (Construction and Use) Regulations 1986 also prohibits the carriage in a minibus of highly inflammable and dangerous substances, unless these are so packed that no damage to the vehicle or injury to passengers is likely to result from an accident involving these substances. Carrying spare fuel in cans inside the vehicle is not acceptable.

Step lights

All steps at passenger exits and gangways must be properly illuminated. The rear exit from a minibus counts as a step for this purpose, even where there is no separate step.

General construction and maintenance

In general all bodywork and fittings must be soundly constructed and maintained in good serviceable condition. Operators should therefore check periodically not only that the above minimum requirements are still being met by their vehicle, but also that seats are clean and not torn, there are no sharp or dangerous projections in the vehicle, windows are clean and floor coverings are not dangerously worn.

Equipment and specification of the vehicle

As well as complying with all the above statutory fitness regulations, there are further matters to which operators and prospective purchasers of minibuses should have regard. These include the equipment which the vehicle must carry, the type of fuel to be used and the transmission to be fitted.

Schedule 7, fire and first aid equipment required to be carried

The 1986 Construction and Use Regulations require every minibus first used on or after 1.4.88 to carry a fire extinguisher and first aid box. The earlier Minibus Regulations of 1977 contained an almost identical requirement in respect of older minibuses.

Both the extinguisher and the contents of the box require regular checking to ensure that they still comply with schedule 7 of the Construction and Use Regulations, which prescribes the British Standard (Number BS 5423 1980 as amended in April 1984) with which the extinguisher should comply and the minimum contents of the first aid box.

The extinguisher may contain water, foam or halon. If the latter, this must be clearly marked.

The first aid box must contain:

(a) ten foil wrapped antiseptic wipes;
(b) one conforming disposable bandage at least 7.5 cm wide;
(c) two triangular bandages;
(d) one packet of 24 assorted adhesive dressings;
(e) three large sterile unmedicated ambulance dressings at least 15 × 20 cm;
(f) two sterile eye pads with attachments;
(g) twelve assorted safety pins;
(h) one pair of rustless and blunt edged scissors.

Propulsion

Petrol

Petrol, or internal combustion, engines have always been thought to be the natural choice of power unit for relatively light vehicles.

In general a petrol engine gives better acceleration than a diesel unit and a smoother and quieter ride, and is considered to be better where frequent stopping and starting is required.

Diesel

However, today's small diesel is a viable alternative to a petrol engine. Many medium sized cars are now fitted with compression ignition (diesel) engines which give performances not much different to their petrol engine counterparts.

The initial cost can be substantially greater but compression ignition engines give improved fuel and maintenance economy which can more than pay for itself over the vehicle's life. In addition they do not produce dangerous lead fumes. Diesel fuel is prone to waxing in cold weather and may need mixing with expensive additives to prevent this, although some oil companies have taken steps to improve the performance of their products in this respect.

LPG

In the United Kingdom the cost of diesel fuel is not substantially different to that of petrol but liquid petroleum gas (LPG) is considerably cheaper. Even allowing for the slightly lower miles per gallon obtained, it is estimated that a LPG conversion should pay for itself after 17,000 miles. Thereafter considerable operating savings can be made.

If necessary, the driver can switch from LPG to petrol during journeys. In an accident, the LPG pressure vessel is generally safer than a petrol tank. However, minibuses which use LPG, even if only for heating, must be fitted with valves which cut off the supply if the vehicle tilts more than 35 degrees.

Electric vehicles

Electric vehicles are a further possibility but they have limited range (about 60 miles between rechargings) and a low maximum speed of approximately 40 mph. They can be a viable alternative for intensive local urban work of a short duration, such as a peak hour inter station link, or a local dial-a-ride Community Transport service where high speeds are unlikely. Electric vehicles are silent, smooth, give good acceleration, have few maintenance problems and are virtually pollution free. With fuel costs about 25% of those of conventional vehicles they are cheap to operate but tend to have correspondingly higher capital costs.

Transmissions

Transmissions, including clutch and gearbox, frequently fail on minibuses, especially in stop start usage. A solution is to specify an automatic transmission which can actually return better mileage figures in urban driving, although slightly higher fuel consumption might be noticed on long fast trips. A fifth gear on a manual gearbox is useful if the minibus is to be used frequently over long distances.

Heaters

A further waste of fuel arises from the use of the engine to operate the heater when the vehicle is stationary. Fitting a proprietory independent heater can offer considerable savings if this is a problem for the operator.

Retarders

Savings on replacement brake linings and pads can also be made by specifying retarders, either the mechanical type which work through the gearbox or the electrical type which operate on the transmission line. An exhaust brake can also achieve a similar effect. Where operations are in hilly terrain, or involve frequent braking as on hail and ride services, this is an option well worth considering especially on the larger, heavier minibuses and midis.

Use of the vehicle

Taxation

Many minibuses are registered as private light goods vehicles and attract the same vehicle excise duty (VED) as a private car.

However, where a minibus is only used on a chargeable basis, for example by a PSV operator under a PSV O licence, by a Community Transport operator under a Permit or as a Community Bus with a Community Bus Permit, it may be taxed at the Hackney Carriage rate applicable to vehicles which ply for hire. This is based on seating capacity and for a minibus is approximately half the private light goods rate.

No VED is payable on certain welfare vehicles used to transport sick and disabled persons to and from hospitals and other medical and welfare centres. These must have the word AMBULANCE painted on the side, which serves to identify their non tax status and legitimise their lack of a tax disc.

Car tax is a form of purchase tax levied on minibuses with less than 12 passenger seats, payable when the vehicle is purchased new or when it is converted to this class. VAT is also charged on new vehicles. Both taxes, or, where applicable, VAT only, can be avoided if the minibus has the status of an ambulance.

This is different from ambulance status for VED purposes (the criteria are much stricter) the vehicle having to be signed as an ambulance and to carry a BSI 7 foot 6 inch stretcher which can be loaded with a patient into, and secured in, the vehicle. There must also be at least one seat for an attendant in the compartment behind the driver.

"Accessible vehicles" designed or substantially or permanently adapted for the safe carriage of handicapped persons in wheelchairs may also be zero rated for VAT purposes. They may be buses or minibuses and do not need to be signed as ambulances, a useful concession since some disabled passengers feel that riding in an "ambulance" is mildly insulting.

Tests on minibuses

Most minibuses used as PSVs are subject to the Class VI MOT test for PSVs. Permit minibuses with more than 16 seats also have been tested to PSV fitness standards.

However, buses used as PSVs which do not need a Certificate of Initial Fitness take the less stringent Class V test. These would include Local Education Authority vehicles and Community Buses. (The Public Passenger Vehicles Act 1981 requires all PSVs with more than eight seats to either have a Certificate of Initial Fitness issued by a certifying officer of the Department of Transport, or be "type approved" by the Department.)

Class VI tests are only conducted at HGV testing stations or on certain large designated operators' premises.

Minibuses with more than 12 passenger seats (including Permit minibuses and personnel carriers – private vehicles belonging to firms and providing free travel) and those PSVs mentioned above which do not need a Certificate of Initial Fitness are subject to a Class V MOT test which can only be carried out at HGV test stations, by designated local councils and at a very few "Department of Transport franchised" MOT testing stations which have the facilities to examine larger vehicles. The test and the certificate are identical to the ordinary MOT test and certificate.

Operators submitting Class V vehicles to MOT test stations must ensure that these have the authority to conduct such tests.

Minibuses with more than eight but less than twelve passenger seats may be given a normal MOT test, but the date on which they become due for such a test is one year (not three years as with cars) from the date they are first used.

Class	Non PSV	PSVs	First examination after	Examined by		
				DTp	Authorised examiner	Designated council
IV	eight or less seats	eight or less seats	three years	×	√	√
	more than eight but less than 13 seats		one year	×	√	√
V	More than 12 seats★ including work buses and "Permit minibuses"	PSVs with *no* CIF, ie Community Buses, LEA's school buses	one year	√	Å	√
VI		PSVs with more than eight seats not in class V	one year	√	–	–

Å Only a few authorised examiners have the facilities to test Class V vehicles and are authorised to do so.
× There is a public Department of Transport testing facility at Hendon.
★ Excluding the driver's seat.

Accidents

Whenever an accident occurs involving the vehicle on a road, the driver must immediately stop and report any damage caused to property (including other vehicles or property on or immediately adjacent to the road) or to certain animals (including dogs, horses and sheep but not cats), to any person having reasonable grounds for requiring the information. If this cannot be done then the police must be informed as soon as possible and in any case within 24 hours.

The information which must be exchanged with the driver of any other vehicle involved in the accident is the name and address of the driver (and the owner of the vehicle if the driver is not the owner) and the vehicle registration number and details of insurance.

Failure to stop or report an accident is an offence.

Insurance

The Road Traffic Act 1972 provides that every motor vehicle used on a road must be covered by insurance in respect of injury to, or damage to property owned by, any third party. A third party insurance policy must also provide cover in respect of any liability for death or personal injury to passengers in the vehicle and any emergency medical treatment arising from an accident.

A third party insurance can be extended, although this is not a legal requirement, to a comprehensive policy covering damage to the insured vehicle and its driver. It is a wise precaution to do this.

Employers must also take out employer liability insurance to cover their staff, and would be wise also to arrange cover for public liability, theft of their revenue by staff (in the form of fidelity guarantees) and personal accident insurance in respect of their employees.

The Public Passenger Vehicles Act 1981 makes operators of PSVs absolutely liable for the safety of their passengers.

Production of documents

A certificate of third party insurance must be produced upon request by a police officer, or if this cannot be done immediately, at a nominated police station within seven days. Unlike ordinary driving licences, which must be produced in person within the same period, the certificate of insurance may be produced on the operator's behalf by another person.

The Road Traffic Act 1988 provides a defence if it can be shown that, due to unforeseen circumstances, it was impossible to produce the document within the stipulated time and it was produced as soon as was reasonably possible.

A PSV driver's licence must also be produced on demand to a police officer, certifying officer or PSV examiner within seven days (when required by a police officer) or within ten days when required to be produced to the Department of Transport.

Operators' responsibility

Safety is paramount; this is not only a moral imperative but also a legal one. Failure to observe the safety requirements outlined in this chapter and provide the guarantee of quality that passengers are entitled to expect can have serious economic consequences. It may ultimately lead to the loss of an O licence or Permit: literally the end of the road for that person.

CHAPTER 5 *The Deregulated Minibus*

A common misconception about the minibus revolution is that it is a product of deregulation. The Transport and Road Research Laboratory report on urban minibuses gives the lie to this:

> Minibuses are not new and have been used in both rural and urban settings, in the case of the latter in specialised niches or on short term experimental bases.
>
> The deployment of minibuses in Exeter in 1984 marked a radical departure from previous experience in so far as they replaced conventional buses with higher frequency services.
>
> Since Exeter the deployment of minibuses has been rapid. National Bus Company subsidiaries have been the prime movers, although other operators are developing interest.

The year before the now well reported "Exeter experiment", a rather less well publicised attempt by Mr Anthony Shepherd to create a high frequency minibus service in Greater London was unsuccessful.

Mr Shepherd, who had gained considerable experience of the effects of minibus operation on conventional buses in Hong Kong, proposed to operate two high frequency cross London minibus services using a method "leasing associate". The drivers would not have a contract of employment with Associated Minibus Operators (AMOS, as he styled his proposed enterprise) but would lease the vehicles from AMOS and work to the company timetable. The possibility of such franchised minibus operations post deregulation is discussed in the final chapter.

In order to do this he needed (and until London is deregulated, still would need) the agreement of London Transport Executive (now London Regional Transport). The Executive refused to make such an agreement and the Secretary of State for Transport appointed an inspector to hold an inquiry into an appeal by AMOS against this refusal. The appeal was disallowed for both legal and technical reasons (see Chapter 8). In his conclusions the inspector stated:

> I accept the AMOS view that consideration of their case suffers because it is a subject on which sides are immediately taken. I agree with their point that it is not appropriate to apply conventional bus wisdom to the understanding and acceptance of this new system for

London. There is clearly a wide, almost total divergence of concept and philosophy between the protagonists of the established public transport network and the proposers of an innovative scheme harnessing individual enterprise.

The inspector's words described eloquently the suspicion with which the minibus initiative was viewed in the early 1980s by many in the bus industry. Despite this, there were men of vision within the management of National Bus Company. Advised, it is said, by Mr Shepherd, they played a hunch that in the run up to deregulation the time had come for the minibus.

Deregulation

In July 1984 the Government published a White Paper entitled simply "Buses". It set out the plans to deregulate the industry.

The White Paper pointed out that over 10% of all journeys are made by bus and that 75% of these are for essential purposes: commuting, school, business and shopping. It painted a picture of an industry which had nevertheless declined sadly (by 50% in the last three decades) and was propped up by massive subsidies in the form of revenue support grants made to whole networks of operators' services.

It suggested that existing quantity controls, essentially the Road Service Licensing of bus routes to monopoly operators, should be replaced by an open entry service registration system, where the only controls would be the existing quality operator licensing controls strengthened by additional powers enabling Traffic Commissioners to attach conditions to these licences where operators fail to operate their services as registered or intentionally interfere with another operator's registered service.

The Transport Act 1980 had already deregulated express bus services and created "trial areas" where deregulation had been experimented with on a limited scale. The White Paper commented favourably on the results of trial area deregulation in Hereford.

So far as revenue support was concerned, the Government proposed that this should be limited to supporting those services which the market had failed to provide commercially and which were needed to meet the public transport requirements of an area. PTEs and "Shire Counties" were to put these services out to tender and award service subsidy agreements on the basis of the best value for money.

The White Paper also promised that powers of local authorities to provide concessionary fares schemes would be continued. It proposed, subject to enabling legislation, that taxis should be allowed to carry passengers at separate fares in certain circumstances. Publicly owned passenger transport undertakings were to be either privatised or "hived off" from their then public ownership by PTEs and municipalities into "arms' length" public limited companies. These would be given commercial objectives although for the time being their sole shareholder would be their parent PTE or local authority.

Since the White Paper all National Bus Company subsidiaries have been sold, many to management buyouts. One ex PTE "initial company" has become an Employee Share Ownership PLC (ESOP) and the Secretary of State for Transport has announced the impending sale of Scottish Bus Group.

London was not to be deregulated immediately, although following the break up of the Greater London Council (who were the Passenger Transport Authority for the area) the London Regional Transport Act 1984 had already nationalised London Transport Executive as London Regional Transport (buses and underground) and introduced competitive route tendering.

The distinguishing difference from deregulation in the provinces is that the "winner" of an LRT service subsidy operates under an agreement with LRT without competition (except in the unlikely event of another operator securing a London Local Service Licence on the route).

For the first time the bus industry was to be brought within the scope of competition law.

Special grants towards the capital cost of establishing "innovative" rural bus services were proposed, together with a "transitional" (that is, gradually reducing to zero) additional fuel tax rebate for mileage run on rural services.

From the point of view of minibus operators, paragraph 1.6 of the White Paper is the most interesting.

If the customer has the final say, bus operators will look keenly to see where and when people want to travel. If one operator fails to provide a service that is wanted, another will. They will be stimulated to provide a greater variety of services, using different types of vehicles running on different routes or frequencies, offering more choice to meet peoples' needs. Competing minibuses may offer a fast and frequent service in city centres. Shared taxis may provide transport for people in villages. New services may link residential areas with out of town shopping centres. Operators will not be slow to find out what people want.

The Transport Act 1985

Hot on the heels of the White Paper came a further buses White Paper, then a Bill, followed by the Act, all within the space of one year (1985). D-day (when deregulation was to take effect) was fixed as 26.10.86.

The Act, with some cosmetic amendments (such as the introduction of compulsory participation notices to be served on operators who did not wish to co-operate in concessionary fares schemes) introduced in its hasty passage through Parliament, implemented all of the above provisions.

From the point of view of minibus operators, the following Parts, dealt with in this and the following chapter, were the most significant:

Part	Provision
I	Registration of local service
	Taxis and hire cars
	Permits and other "Section 19" minibuses
	Community Buses
	O licence conditions
II	London Local Service Licence
V	Tendering
	Travel concession schemes
	Rural Passenger Service Grants
	Transitional Rural Bus Grants
VI	Competition law – bus services and bus stations
	Transport tribunal

Local services – control and registration

The Transport Act 1980, which became the Public Passenger Vehicles Act 1981, began the process of deregulation by making "the public interest", rather than the interest of the established operator, the criterion for the grant or refusal of a Road Service Licence.

Complete deregulation came with the Transport Act 1985 which removed from all local services outside London the need for the operator to obtain a Road Service Licence and substituted a simple quality of service control – *registration*. The definition of local service was changed so that 15 miles became the criterion, and by implication, "other" services, including express services, could be run without having to register them.

Local services

A local service is defined as any service operated at separate fares using a PSV on which passengers can make journeys of less than 15 miles measured in a straight line.

Thus a service operating non stop between two points more than 15 miles apart would not be a local service, but the introduction of a midway stop which was within 15 miles of either the starting and finishing points would make it wholly or in part local.

Excursions and tours which take a vehicle more than 15 miles in a straight line from the boarding point are not classed as local, even though passengers will board and alight at the same point. In the same way neither will a service connecting two points less than 15 miles apart in a straight line (for example two towns on either side of an estuary) but which has to travel more than 15 miles in a straight line to do so (for example to reach the lowest crossing point of the estuary) be a local service.

A service can be part local and part "other", as for example if it picks up and sets down at least once in every 15 miles over the first part of the route and then runs non stop to a distant destination, more than 15 miles from the last stop. In such a case only the local part of the service needs to be registered.

London local services

Bus services in London have not yet been deregulated. The system which survives in Greater London under the London Regional Transport Act 1984 is essentially the same as the system of Road Service Licensing which applied throughout the United Kingdom before deregulation.

London Regional Transport may operate a London bus service (a service on which passengers are picked up and set down within Greater London). Other operators, with the agreement of LRT, may also operate a London bus service and may do so either by seeking an agreement with LRT or by running a tendered service for them.

A London Local Service Licence is not required for a London bus service operated in agreement with LRT, in fulfillment of a tendering agreement, for a feeder service linking up with an express service to a place outside Greater London (provided no separate fare is charged for the portion of the service within Greater London), or for an excursion and tour which is not a local service (as defined above).

London Local Service Licences

An operator who does not wish to enter into an operating agreement with LRT to run a London bus service may apply to the Metropolitan Traffic Commissioner for a London Local Service Licence. Application may be made by:

(a) the holder of a PSV O licence, including any suitably licensed minibus operator;
(b) a Local Education Authority proposing to use a school bus to carry fare paying passengers;
(c) the holder of a Community Bus Permit.

The application, which will be published by the Traffic Commissioner in "Notices and Proceedings" and be available for inspection at his or her office, must include such information as:

(a) the route and terminal points (including a map where appropriate);

(b) the period and frequency of the operation, supported by a full timetable if necessary;

(c) route number or service name.

There is no requirement to submit a fare table.

Objections to, and representations against, the application have to be lodged with the Commissioner within 28 days of its publication and a copy sent to the operator. However, the Traffic Commissioner must grant the application unless it appears to him or her that to do so would not be "in the public interest".

The Commissioner must take into account not only any objections and representations but also London's transport needs, the transport policies and plans of the London Boroughs and the City of London and the advice of the Metropolitan Police.

The Commissioner may attach to the licence such *conditions* as he or she thinks necessary to ensure that suitable routes are used, timetables and fare tables are carried on the vehicles, passengers are picked up and set down at defined points and the safety and convenience of the public, including the disabled, is safeguarded.

The normal duration of a London Local Service Licence is five years but the Commissioner may grant an "unforeseen" licence for a shorter period of up to six months without the need to publish details or hear any objections.

An application may also be made to vary an existing licence and such an application is subject to similar rules as to publication and objection. Emergency variations may be made in special circumstances such as a forced sudden route change or an unforeseen change in demand.

The Traffic Commissioner may convene a public inquiry to hear objections to or representations against the application. He or she may also revoke or suspend a London Local Service Licence if the operator contravenes the conditions attached to it.

Appeals against the refusal of the Traffic Commissioner to grant or vary a London Local Service Licence, or his or her revocation, suspension or curtailment of the Licence can be made to the Secretary of State. The operator may request a "stay" of the Commissioner's decision to revoke, suspend or curtail, or not to vary a condition attached to, a London Local Service Licence until the end of the period allowed for appeals.

Persons other than the operator, such as affected local authorities or providers of transport along the route may also appeal to the Secretary of State against the Commissioner's decision in a London Local Service Licence case and further appeals on a point of law only can be made to the High Court.

If a service is to operate partly within Greater London and partly outside, a London Local Service Licence is required for the part within London and the remainder of the service must be registered.

Registration of local services outside London

Registration represents one aspect of deregulation in so far as the regulation of competition by licensing is removed. So long as an operator can find his or her way through the jungle of the PSV (Registration of Local Services) (Amendment) Regulations 1988 there is no bar to operating a local service.

It is, of course, the same for any competitor. These will often be minibus operators, who may come on to a registered route by registering a competing service, even in the case where the original service is provided under a service subsidy agreement with a PTE or Shire County, which the original operator had "won" by competitive tendering.

The registration regulations are in fact even more complex than Road Service Licensing, which they replace. Thus deregulation is a misnomer: decontrol or liberalisation would have been better words.

Registration of a local service implies a commitment to operate this as registered. In fact under the regulations entering a service on a route is actually easier than withdrawing it.

The regulations

Details of all local services (excluding London Local Services) must be registered with the Traffic Commissioners. The following may register a local service:

(a) holders of PSV O licences (including restricted O licences for small passenger carrying vehicles and minibuses and special restricted O licences for taxi operators);

(b) Local Education Authorities using school buses to carry fare paying passengers;

(c) holders of Community Bus Permits.

Applications for registration must be sent to the Traffic Commissioner for the area in which the service is to run (or the area in which it is to start if it will run through more than one area) on form PSV 350. In the case where a service has a stopping place in Greater London the application is sent to the Metropolitan Traffic Commissioner.

The following particulars have to be supplied:

(a) the operator's name and address and O licence/Permit number;

(b) the terminal points;

(c) whether the service is an excursion or tour;

(d) the route, stops (or parts of route where "hail and ride" operate) and turning arrangements at route ends;

(e) the commencement date;

(f) the timetable.

It is no longer necessary to state the largest capacity of vehicle to be used on the service.

Applications to register, vary or cancel a local service must be *accepted* by the Traffic Commissioner not less than 42 days prior to implementation. The word accepted causes some difficulties; it does not mean received. As a consequence of this some operators have already found themselves in the position of believing that they can commence a service on a certain date, only to discover that because of a technical irregularity in their registration, they must commence later.

If publicity is already prepared this can be embarrassing but it is still open to the operator to run the service as an unregistered "free" service to generate traffic in the few days running up to the registration date.

No period of notice at all is required to:

(a) register a service requiring a London Local Service Licence for part of the route so long as application for the Licence and registration and the implementation of both are simultaneous;

(b) provide a rail replacement service;

(c) vary a registration as a result of a traffic regulation condition.

Service variations in weeks containing public holidays

Services may be varied without having to alter the registration in England and Wales where journeys take place in all or part of a week which includes certain specified public holidays but operators must send to the local authority and the Traffic Commissioner notice of their intention to vary their service at least 21 days before this is to take effect.

This "second tier" notification is not a variation of a registration requiring the filling in of forms and the payment of fees but it is legally enforceable.

The Traffic Commissioner may, at his or her discretion, determine a shorter period of notice in certain cases including:

(a) registration/variation of an existing service by an operator to provide a substantially similar replacement for a service which *either he or* another operator has withdrawn (the words in italics were inserted in the amendment to the regulations to allow the same operator to re-register his or her service at short notice if he or she re-commences it under a service subsidy agreement);

(b) variation/cancellation of a service (for example, serving a school or works) not available to or not regularly used by the public;

(c) variation/cancellation resulting from a representation concerning road safety or a traffic regulation condition made by a traffic authority or the police;

(d) a new or augmented service to be operated over not more than 21 days in connection with a special event or occasion;

(e) an insignificant change of timetable of up to plus or minus 10 minutes or to provide a rail, ferry or air service connection;

(f) variation or suspension of not more than 14 days to cover local holidays;

(g) where unforeseen circumstances prevent the operator giving 42 days' notice of a variation or application;

(h) registration or variation of a service or part of a service to meet an urgent and exceptional public transport requirement.

Changes to registered services

Some modifications can be made to registered services without the need for the operator to apply for a variation to the registration.

Traffic Commissioners can also terminate a registered service which has become discontinued as a result of the operator ceasing to trade. They may do so immediately if the operator dies or loses his or her O licence, or when a company or partnership is dissolved.

In any other case they will be able to serve a notice on the operator that unless a response is received within 28 days, they will cancel the registration.

The other cases where modifications can be made without the need to vary the registration are listed below:

(a) Where a journey is retimed by no more than five minutes. (Thus a service with a 10 minute frequency can be registered without a timetable, an extremely useful provision in relation to the running of high frequency urban minibus services.)

(b) Where a registered excursion or tour is withdrawn or cancelled. (Excursions and tours which are local services need only be registered if they are to be operated one or more times per week for a continuous period of six weeks.)

(c) A route change to incorporate a temporary diversion (eg for road works).

(d) A change of route number or service name (since these particulars do not need to be registered).

(e) Where a school service provided by a Local Education Authority and not available to the public is varied temporarily to enable the LEA to fulfil its duty to provide free transport. (A simple example would be where a school finished early.)

(f) Where the operator provides additional vehicles which:

(i)   are operated over any part of the route or service and,

(ii) are operated as closely as possible to the timings in the timetable.

This last case, which was only added by the 1988 Amending Regulations, concerns *duplication*.

The amended regulations do not clarify the issue of whether an operator must justify passenger demand for an additional vehicle, or run this ahead of the timetabled service. An empty minibus slipped in front of a competitor's service can be seen as predatory duplication or effective competition, depending on the observer's viewpoint.

Operators who do this will continue to be referred to the Traffic Commissioner by their competitors for intentionally interfering with a registered service but it is uncertain what the outcome of such a referral might be under the amended regulations.

Joint or shared services

These may either be registered by one operator acting as co-ordinator of the service or by each operator registering his or her part of the service.

Joint services may also be subject to a quite different form of additional registration with the Office of Fair Trading, which has nothing to do with registering a local service but relates to competition law; this is dealt with later in the chapter.

Copies of applications to register, vary or cancel a service must be sent to affected PTEs and County, Regional or Island Councils as the case may be. The Traffic Commissioner publishes details of applications received and accepted in "Notices and Proceedings".

Destination indicators must be displayed clearly on the exterior of vehicles operating registered local services and faretables and timetables must be displayed or otherwise made available to passengers.

Operators may charge whatever fares they see fit on commercially registered services but on tendered services the service subsidy agreement may restrict this freedom by, for example, stipulating a maximum fare and/or a requirement to accept scholars passes.

Fees payable are:
(a)   registration of a local service £30;
(b)   variation of a local service £27.

No fee is payable to register a service requiring a London Local Service Licence, or to vary a service to comply with a traffic regulation condition.

Operating "as registered"

The Public Passenger Vehicles Act 1981 has always allowed Traffic Commissioners to attach conditions to an O licence. These might include the maximum number and type of vehicles to be specified, the places where these may pick up and set down, and that the operator complies with the Sporting Events (Control of Alcohol) Act 1985.

The Transport Act 1985, in adding to this list, allows Commissioners to attach what have become known as section 26 conditions, section 111 conditions and traffic regulation conditions.

Section 26 conditions

These allow a Commissioner to prohibit an operator from providing any (or a specified) registered local service where it appears to him or her that the operator has:

    (a)   run an unregistered local service;

    (b)   failed to run a registered local service or not run it as registered, or run it in a dangerous manner;

    (c)   failed to maintain his or her vehicles satisfactorily;

or that he or she, or an employee or agent has intentionally interfered in the running of another operator's local service.

The Traffic Commissioner may also restrict the vehicles to be used under the licence to specified ones.

In deciding whether to impose a section 26 condition the Commissioner will take account of whether the operator's conduct was reckless or intentional, the frequency of the misconduct and the danger to the public.

S. 111 Penalties

This enables the Commissioner to reduce by 20% the fuel tax rebate granted to an operator during a three month period if that operator can be shown to have operated a registered local service unreliably or not in accordance with the registered details or to have failed to register his or her operations.

Traffic Regulation Conditions (TRC)

The Transport Act 1985 allowed Traffic Commissioners to attach conditions affecting the operation of local services to O licences. They may only take this action if requested to do so by an appropriate traffic authority, which the PSV (Traffic Regulation Conditions) Regulation 1986 defines as a Metropolitan District Council, a Shire Council or, in Scotland, a Regional or Island Council.

The Commissioner may only consider attaching a TRC either to reduce severe congestion or to prevent danger to road users. He or she must take account of the interest of operators and users of local services and of elderly and disabled persons.

Conditions may relate to routes, stops and layover times, or indeed any other relevant matters and may apply to all services or a specified service.

Unless the Traffic Commissioner thinks it is necessary to introduce the TRC urgently and immediately he or she must, if an operator of a local service or the traffic authority requests it, first hold a public inquiry.

Even where the Commissioner has already introduced a TRC, he or she must still hold an inquiry if so requested. The Commissioner can also revoke a TRC on request from a traffic authority or the operator of a local service if he or she sees fit to do so.

Details of every request for a determination, variation or revocation of a TRC are published in "Notices and Proceedings", together with at least 28 days' notice of any public inquiry concerning them.

Appeals against the imposition of a TRC, its variation or revocation, or the refusal of a Commissioner to vary or revoke it, must be made to the Secretary of State and received by him or her within 28 days of the Traffic Commissioner's determination or refusal. Further appeals, on points of law only, lie with the High Court.

Bus stations

Some minibus operators, such as many of the ex National Bus Company subsidiaries, enjoy rights of access to local bus stations simply because they own them.

The Transport Act 1985 made Passenger Transport Authorities which were bus operators before deregulation and had bus stations, the operators of these premises. Those municipalities which were in a similar position before deregulation also became the operators of their bus stations by this Act. However, it made a further provision that they were not to discriminate against any operators in the operation of a bus station in their areas or in relation to departure charges for their vehicles.

Bus stations are also brought within the ambit of competition law (considered below).

Minibus operators have to decide whether they wish their services to operate from or through the town bus station, or whether they feel that they can gain a competitive advantage by penetrating further into the commercial centre of the town than is possible with conventional buses. Of course they may attempt to do both simultaneously.

Avoidance of the bus station saves departure charges, but also denies the operator transfer traffic from other services. On the other hand, calling at the bus station after circling the town may be unproductive if the minibus is already full by then.

Use of a bus station can avoid delays caused by congestion and it can be a useful transfer point, not only between an operator's own minibus services but also with competitors' services. In the end, it is the operator's commercial judgement which will decide the optimum strategy.

If operators consider bus station charges unreasonable they can apply to the Traffic Commissioner who will review them and if he or she thinks that the owner of the bus station is engaging in anti-competitive practices, the matter can be referred to the Office of Fair Trading (OFT), as described in the next section. Operators may also complain to the Traffic Commissioner of any other practice which they consider prejudicial to them. Already, complaints of one operator "blocking in" another in a bus station, or occupying another's stand have been heard by Traffic Commissioners.

Competition law

The Transport Act 1985 brought the bus industry into line with other industries by ending its various exemptions from competition legislation. The Act also applied the law on restrictive agreements, contained in the Restrictive Trade Practices Act 1976, to bus services.

The 1985 Act extended the application of the law on anti-competitive practices, as contained in the Competition Act 1980, to the operation of bus stations as well as to bus services.

Bus service monopolies

Before the Transport Act 1985 the Secretary of State for Trade and Industry could, using powers under the Competition Act 1980, make most large passenger transport undertakings the subject of a reference to the Monopolies and Mergers Commission on questions of efficiency, costs, services, or the likely abuse of their local monopoly.

The Act now removes from nearly all of the industry any possibility that this might happen. Such references can now only be made in respect of the nationalised parts of the industry.

Monitoring possible monopoly situations

The Director General of the Office of Fair Trading has a duty to keep possible monopoly situations under review and refer them to the Monopolies and Mergers Commission for investigation. A monopoly is where one operator controls or acquires 25% or more of the supply of services in the United Kingdom or part of it.

Restrictive agreements

The provisions of the Restrictive Trade Practices Act 1976 now apply to all operators, including operators of bus stations. A restrictive agreement is one made between two or more operators in which they accept any limitations on their ability to compete.

Such agreements must be registered with the OFT within three months of the agreement being made and before it comes into effect. If this is not done the agreement becomes legally void and unlawful to operate and anyone harmed by the restriction can sue for damages.

This is the "other type" of registration referred to earlier in the context of the registration of a joint local service by the co-ordinating partner in the service. Since both parties are effectively agreeing to co-operate rather than compete, this agreement must be registered with the OFT, as well as the service being registered with the Traffic Commissioner.

Restrictive agreements are not automatically illegal. Provided details are properly furnished to the OFT in advance they can continue to operate. Once an agreement is registered the Director General must refer this to the Restrictive Practices Court, which will consider whether it appears to be "against the public interest".

There is no penalty if an agreement is ruled against but to re-register the same or a very similar agreement would certainly be considered by the court which found against it as contempt.

The Director General of the OFT can recommend to the Secretary of State for Trade and Industry that the restrictions are not significant enough to be referred to the Restrictive Practices Court.

In deciding whether or not an agreement is significant the Director General will, in general, have regard to:

(a)   the extent to which the operators face external competition;
(b)   the bargaining strength of the parties in the market;
(c)   the clarity and reasonableness of the standard trading terms and conditions of the operators' trade association, if the agreement is based on these.

Public interest

The law makes the assumption that all restrictive agreements are against the public interest, unless the contary can be proved. Agreements which can satisfy various tests (described as "gateways") designed to show that they are not against the public interest will not be "struck down" by the Restrictive Practices Court.

The most useful gateway in the Restrictive Trade Practices Act is that "the removal of the restriction would deny the public substantial benefits and advantages". This test might be applied to "let through", joint ticketing arrangements where operators agree to accept each others' tickets, even though such an agreement contains an element of fare fixing.

"Registerable" agreements

The Restrictive Trade Practices Act 1976 lists six kinds of agreements which could be considered restrictive and hence registerable. The examples given in brackets show how almost any operating agreement can be construed in this way.

(a)   Provision of services (eg joint operation).

(b) Prices (eg fares, joint tendering, revenue pooling, ticket interavailability).
(c) Terms and conditions (eg picking up and setting down restrictions).
(d) Areas of operation (eg attempts to "carve up" a district between friendly operators, sometimes referred to as market sharing).
(e) Scale of operation (eg any limits agreed on level of competition).
(f) Persons dealt with (eg agreements to accept only one operator's return tickets).

Probably agreements between operators to fix fares or not to compete with each other on a particular route or in a particular area will be seen as restrictive.

However, an agreement within an operators' panel to continue travel cards and multi journey ticket arrangements which existed before deregulation would probably be let through but much would depend on the fairness of the revenue sharing agreement, the extent to which all operators in the area are free to join in and whether any obvious collusion to fix fares is taking place within the panel.

Agreements relating to the pre-sale of tickets off-bus are further discussed in Chapter 6.

Some "restrictive" agreements, such as joint operation on a common headway, as well as making commercial sense, contain decided advantages and benefits to the public and would thus appear to satisfy the gateway criterion of public benefit.

Anti-competitive practices

The Competition Act 1980 already applies to the bus industry, but the Transport Act 1985 now brings bus stations within its scope. Any conduct by an operator or by an operator and other persons which has or is intended or likely to have the effect of restricting or distorting competition can be held to be anti-competitive.

The Competition Act has to be read in conjunction with the Transport Act 1985 which provide that PTEs and local authorities must not inhibit competition in the way in which they manage access to their bus stations.

The OFT can investigate a practice to determine whether it is anti-competitive, although (with a few exceptions) they can only do so if the operator(s) in question controls over 25% of the market concerned. They discuss the matter with the operator(s), looking at the market affected and taking account of their market power.

Predatory pricing

The OFT has to try to ascertain the intentions behind any questionable operating practices. For example, if they are investigating predatory pricing (charging fares below cost or giving free transport) they have to decide whether the operator is doing this as a loss leader to become known on a route and create a brand loyalty, or to force the competition off the route.

If the OFT find that the practice is anti-competitive they can accept an undertaking from the operator to drop it but if this is not obtained, they can then refer the case to the Monopolies and Mergers Commission.

The Commission will then establish that the practice actually is anti-competitive and decide whether it is against the public interest. If its report contains an adverse finding the Secretary of State can make an order banning the practice.

The reality is that the Director General of the Office of Fair Trading is now, even more so than the Traffic Commissioner (who is concerned with safety and reliability), the arbiter of fair competition on the buses. The OFT's address is: Field House, 15–25 Breams Buildings, London EC4A 1PR.

Minibus operators who might feel that their local large bus operator is competing unfairly against them have a champion to whom to turn. Shortly after deregulation a minibus operator who was refused access to a bus station owned by the large operator who had up until then enjoyed a monopoly of services in the area complained to the OFT with favourable (to him) results.

Making a complaint

However, it should be borne in mind that when a complaint about a competitor is made, whether to the Traffic Commissioner or the OFT, the complainant should ensure that his or her own hands are clean! In both instances, as this chapter has shown, the process of investigation is not only fair, but extremely rigorous.

CHAPTER 6 *Pricing and Costing*

The cost of operating minibuses

Typically a minibus with 25 seats costs around £18,500, a single-deck conventional bus (Leyland National) around £55,000 and a conventional one man double-deck vehicle around £61,500.

A formula much quoted in bus operating circles is £1000 per seat and whilst there are quite wide variations on this theme, it does provide a reasonable costing rule of thumb.

If frequencies are trebled on a route it would be possible to substitute three minibuses for each conventional bus replaced. In fact, looking at some of NBC's conversions the replacement ratio of buses to minibuses, originally planned at about 3.5:1 has settled down at about 2.5:1.

Maintenance costs rise steeply after the early warranty years. Three drivers are needed to replace one driver of a conventional bus.

The life of a minibus is less than half that of a conventional bus. At present this is the big question mark in minibus costing. Much depends on the specification of the original vehicle. As with private cars, whilst the capital cost of a Mercedes will be greater than a Ford, its operational life expectancy will be longer. As pointed out in Chapter 4, the minibus revolution has been accompanied by an evolution of design and it can be expected that the later fleet of larger heavier PSV specification vehicles will outlast the original van conversions which heralded the revolution.

Six years is a typical average life span for a minibus currently being suggested by the chief engineers of undertakings with large fleets of these. Many of these engineers have expressed surprise at the durability of some vehicles which they had expected to replace much sooner.

Although the operators could be buying two, or even three, generations of minibuses within the life of a conventional bus, they do make some short term capital savings which can improve cash flow just at the point in their operations when they may need every penny to adjust to the new competitive environment. It is also easier to match vehicle supply to traffic demand if replacement policy is to exchange vehicles more frequently than before.

Spares for minibuses, which are often derivatives of commercial vehicles, are usually available off the shelf at local agents so there is a saving in the cost of stock carried. In fact many minibus operators rely on local agents to carry out all but the most basic maintenance and repairs, thus saving many engineering overheads.

Costs fall into two headings, those variable costs associated with the running of the vehicle, and fixed or standing costs which are incurred with time irrespective of mileage.

Variable costs

These include fuel, oil and tyre costs, all of which vary directly in proportion to the vehicle mileage. The type of operation, whether hilly, in heavy traffic or on empty rural roads will also have a marginal effect on things like fuel consumption and tyre wear.

It would be misleading in a book of this nature to quote actual costs, since these differ enormously between operators and with time. A useful source of up to date costing information is Croner's "Operational Costings for Transport Management", which is looseleaf and is updated twice annually.

Actual fuel costs incurred are much less in the case of minibuses used to provide a registered local service, since these attract Fuel Duty Rebate, and, when operated on rural services, the transitional Rural Bus Grant.

The following figures were given in "Coachmart and Bus Operator" in Autumn 1988 and will illustrate this point.

FUEL CONSUMPTION	REBATE IN PENCE PER MILE	
	Rural miles	Urban miles
10 mpg	13.33	9.83
16 mpg	8.41	4.91

(Between 1989–92 the rebate will be progressively reduced for rural operation until it is the same as that for urban operation.)

Minibuses used by schools, Community Transport and other non PSV operators will not receive any Fuel Duty Rebate and their fuel costs could be as high as 17p per mile (assuming a fuel consumption of 10 mpg).

Maintenance costs vary with mileage where this is carried out on the basis of regular inspections and services every so many miles. Repairs after accidents and breakdowns are sometimes dealt with as a fleet overhead and described as workshop expenses. The vehicle's annual freedom from defect inspection by the DTp is definitely an overhead which occurs every 12 months irrespective of mileage.

Even where operators do not carry out their own inspections, maintenance and repairs but contract them out to a garage, they are still responsible for ensuring that they are done to the standards required of the holder of an O licence. If they are not, it is their licences which are at risk.

Labour

There is some debate as to whether labour costs are fixed or variable. To the extent that an operator employs a permanent work force, they must be fixed at least in the short term but, on the other hand, the cost of casual labour (such as part time drivers) and overtime payments may be considered as variable.

The TRRL Report on NBC urban minibuses found that minibus driver costs were substantially lower than those for full sized buses due to lower basic rates, more flexible scheduling, lower overtime rates and simpler shift patterns. Recruitment at lower wage rates (in 1986/7 when the report was prepared and written) had been possible due to current high unemployment levels.

Ironically, most of the NBC experimental minibus networks surveyed were in the South of England, where there are signs of the economy overheating in the late 1980s, so that this assumption may not be true for long. Already, undertakings in London and the South East are reporting recruitment difficulties.

Again, although it is misleading to quote figures which so quickly become outdated, the study identified rates of pay for minibus drivers of between £2.30 and £3.00 per hour, which were then some 20% below conventional bus one person operator rates. However, reference has already been made to the upward pressure on minibus drivers' rates from the improvement of some local labour markets and the attempts by some managements to secure single status wage agreements giving flexibility of employment of staff between different sizes of vehicles.

Fixed costs

These include taxation of the vehicle (including the fee for an O licence and road fund tax — fuel tax being considered a running cost), depreciation, insurance and "establishment costs". Labour is also a fixed cost with any period of guaranteed employment (eg the working day).

Depreciation is based on capital costs. The amount written off annually depends on the life of the vehicle and the method of depreciation used. A reducing balance method writes off the heaviest amounts in the early years of the vehicle, when repair and maintenance costs might be expected to be least. Thus the total of these two taken together should be fairly stable at net present values (that is, making no allowance for inflation).

A fixed line method is simplest, where the cost of the vehicle less its residual value is divided by its life and the amount written off annually, but it can give a distorted view of the value of the vehicle in the operator's books.

Perhaps the most reliable way is to employ current cost accounting methods and depreciate by the difference between the cost and replacement cost, updating the figures annually.

Employing discounted cash flow techniques it can be shown that by acquiring three vehicles over the lifetime of a conventional vehicle where the sum of the costs of the three vehicles is the same as the cost of the conventional one, operators can dramatically improve their cash flow position. This is just one of the "hidden accounting pluses" of minibus operation.

Allocation of costs

There are some costs which can be considered to be semi variable in so far as they do not vary in the short term in proportion to time or mileage operated.

These costs have to be apportioned on the basis of sharing them amongst the number of vehicles required to provide a given level of service, the so called peak vehicle requirement. Arguably, they "stand on the books", even during the off peak period. They include most establishment costs, such as publicity, administrative and management, training, buildings and, a cost often overlooked, the provision, upkeep and repair of on-bus ticket machines.

Marginal costs

In an ideal world every job would produce sufficient revenue to cover not only the direct running costs associated with it but also all of its assessed contribution to the undertaking's fixed costs.

However, where a vehicle and staff are available and would otherwise not be used, it can make commercial sense, at least in the short term, to allocate them to work which produces sufficient revenue to cover their direct costs *and makes some contribution to overheads*. This is the rationale behind providing minibuses at night and weekends for private hire jobs. So long as fuel and labour costs are covered, any surplus revenue goes to increasing the undertaking's profits, and reducing unit costs.Conversely, the removal of marginally remunerative mileage increases unit costs and, if average cost is the criterion, leads to another round of self-defeating cuts.

Prices and fares

The price which a minibus operator charges his or her passengers, whether in the form of separate fares on a registered local service or as a composite charge for his or her vehicle under a private hire contract will depend on a variety of factors.

The operator may base the charges on the full cost of the operation plus a mark up for profit, or, as explained above, on his or her marginal costs and a contribution to the overheads.

The operator may also be influenced by the charges made by competitors. There may also be an element of averaging in his or her charges, so that provided the average fare is sufficient to meet costs, some passengers, typically "short riders", will subsidise others such as those travelling the full length of a route.

Finally, the operator may decide to resort to the pricing system known as "charging what the traffic will bear". In other words, if he or she has a monopoly on a route, or provides a "premium" service, such as an express airport link, he or she may feel that it is possible to extract a higher fare than on a service where there is competition. Of course, in doing so, the operator invites competition!

Fares

The TRRL report noted that "in general, fare levels have remained unchanged upon minibus introduction, as have child and OAP concessions. Unlimited use tickets (travelcards) are often simultaneously introduced partly to offset fare penalties on interchange".

The early fears of operators that minibuses would develop into a premium service higher fare network have not been realised. This is because they have been able to generate extra traffic to compensate for the overall higher costs of a minibus conversion scheme.

The commonest fare system employed on minibus routes is still the traditional United Kingdom tapered fare scale. This is based on a fare proportional to distance travelled but the fare steps or stages being tapered so that longer distance passengers effectively pay less per mile travelled than short distance passengers. The fare scale is said to ripple outwards.

It is of course perfectly feasible to taper a fare scale in the opposite direction, the so called ripple inwards concept, to encourage short riders and some minibus operators do have a short hop low fare.

Some area-wide ticketing and fares schemes provide for zonal fares in which passengers purchase travelcards or multi journey tickets (which they cancel once for each trip on the vehicles) valid within a zone or between one, two or more zones. The Dutch National Strippenkarten scheme where a passenger cancels one strip on the ticket on boarding the vehicle plus one additional strip for every zone traversed is an excellent example of such a scheme.

Within small market towns not large enough to be divided into zones, or with short cross town routes, a simple solution to average pricing of the service is to have a flat fare irrespective of distance travelled. A refinement of this is to recharge passengers on cross town services once they pass through the central area.

Return tickets are a means of generating passenger loyalty, ensuring that they do not catch a competitor's service on the return trip. However, many operators feel that the benefits of accepting each other's return tickets will, on balance, generate more traffic for everyone and result in higher revenues.

Providing that everyone's services are fairly evenly balanced, the simplest revenue pooling agreement in this case is for each operator to retain the revenue for the tickets which he or she sells. Agreements as to mutual recognition of other operators' tickets must, of course, be registered with the OFT.

Mention is made later in this chapter of the pre-sale of bus tickets. These may be for specific journeys, like a season ticket, taken over a time period (weekly, monthly or annually), or may be for specific values of travel, like multi journey tickets.

Passengers can be persuaded to purchase in advance, to the benefit of the operator's cash flow, both because discounts are usually offered and because of the convenience of not needing to make a cash transaction on every journey.

The system of selling travel time rather than travel distance has not been adapted in the United Kingdom to the extent that it has on the continent. In many mainland European towns a single flat fare ticket is valid on the whole network for a fixed time, typically two hours, from the purchase time stamped on the ticket by an on-bus cancelling machine.

The DTp are currently sponsoring research into "smart card" travel tickets. The principle could be simply like the telephone cards, where on inserting the card on boarding and then again on alighting the value of the trip is deleted until the card is exhausted.

However, a more exciting development is the idea of the card containing personal details which the cancelling machine would capture so that the passenger could be billed later for journeys taken, rather as people now receive their gas, electric and phone bills. This would do wonders for the passenger's cash flow, but not a lot for the operator's.

Revenue protection

Operators are vulnerable to both passenger and staff dishonesty. Indeed the purpose of a ticket system is not just to give a receipt for the fare paid but to enable the operator to monitor the passenger's journey vis a vis his or her fare and to check the driver's takings against the ticket sales.

The greatest revenue loss experienced with passengers is caused by overriding. The very intimacy of the scale of the minibus means that it is difficult, if not impossible, for a passenger to actually board without paying. One of the operational benefits of minibuses compared to conventional buses is because of their scale and the proximity of driver and passengers, it is also harder for passengers to override if the driver is vigilant.

The use of electronic ticketing machines is widespread nowadays on minibuses. They have a number of advantages over the old conventional manually operated machines, even where these were motor driven.

The data which they provide is much more comprehensive and, being provided on magnetic tapes or EPROM (Eraseable Programable Read Only Memory) or cartridges which can be taken from the machine on the bus at the end of a shift and read by a host computer, they obviate the time consuming ritual of the driver completing a waybill at the end of each service journey.

It is also much more difficult for staff to defraud operators where electronic ticketing is in use since the data collected shows every ticket issued, its value and the stage where issued and is more comprehensive than the fullest audit roles on manual ticket machines.

The comprehensive data provided by electronic ticketing machines is also of enormous use to an operator in devising a marketing strategy. There is more information on this in Chapter 7.

Finally, the data collected represents 100% of the undertaking's passengers and is much more reliable for the purposes of estimating the operator's "take" from a concessionary fare scheme or an off bus ticket sales pool. For this reason some Passenger Transport Authorities are presently considering using powers given to them in the Transport Act 1985 to purchase electronic ticketing machines for use on their tendered services or by operators within concessionary fares schemes.

Off-bus revenue

Revenue which is received on the bus, so called fare box revenue, is not the only source of income to a minibus operator. A relatively small but useful amount of additional income may be generated by carrying advertisements in the saloon and on the outer panels of the minibus, and there are advertising agencies which will handle the whole process, from finding and billing the advertisers to designing and displaying the copy.

The three largest sources of non fare box revenue come from service subsidies obtained by tender, concessionary fare support and off-bus ticket sales.

Tendering

The Transport Act 1985 provides that "authorities responsible for public transport services", called "tendering authorities", can invite tenders for services to meet the public transport requirements of their area so far as these are not being provided by the free market in the form of commercially registered services.

Tendering authorities comprise:

(a)   PTEs in metropolitan areas

(b)   County and District Councils in Shire Counties

(c)   Regional and Island Councils in Scotland

The authorities have certain quite strict duties to observe when carrying out the process of inviting, receiving and letting tenders.

First of all, they must not act in any way which might "inhibit competition". Thus it could be argued that putting out a whole block of services to tender, no matter how interwoven these have been in the past, could inhibit a small operator with limited resources from bidding, whilst simultaneously favouring a large established operator, who possibly even operated these services in the past. Even asking for tenders to provide a greater frequency on a commercial route could be construed as inhibiting competition. Large and small minibus operators alike should consider these points as both may bear on their services.

Secondly they have a duty to co-operate with Local Education Authorities and social services departments so as to obtain the best value for ratepayers' money. Free transport for children living more than three miles from school, for example, can be provided by either requiring the operator winning the tender to accept free passes or by purchasing passes from the same or another operator of a convenient commercial service.

Finally, in exercising their duty to consider tenders on the basis of "best value for money", tendering authorities will inevitably have to include in their calculations any expenditure on related services. Thus an operator proposing to link two or more services in order to effect operating economies and thus put in a price for both lower than the sum of the lowest individual tenders will probably be awarded both services even if his or her individual tenders are undercut.

Tendering must be *open*, that is there can be no pre-qualification such as a requirement that operators observe locally negotiated wages and conditions of service but the Act does specify that contracts can only be let to holders of PSV O licences and Community Bus Permits. The maximum length of a contract is five years.

Types of tender

There are two basic types of tender, plus a third hybrid type. The simplest of these is what has become known as the *"fixed cost" or supply side tender*. Operators are asked to say what would be the cost to them of operating the service assuming the authority kept the revenue. Once such a tender is won, there is no further risk to the operator, even if a competitor comes on the route. The authority sets the fares and has to make sure that the operator collects all revenue due and accounts for this.

Since the fares do not represent the operator's own money there is little incentive to discourage fare dodgers. In short, the authority takes most of the risks. However, one risk the authority will normally avoid is that the operator will invoke a break clause and leave them with no service to meet their obligations.

The other type of tender has become known as the *"bottom line" or net subsidy* tender. In this instance operators are asked to state their price for providing the service on the assumption that they will keep all the revenue. The authority usually sets a maximum fare but operators are free to devise their own pricing policy within this headroom. They will have every incentive to maximise their revenue from the service, since they risk not covering their costs otherwise. They run the risk of revenue shortfall and of new competition appearing.

Some authorities invite operators to put in tenders on either basis. The advantages and disadvantages of each type are summarised in the table below.

Type of tender	Supply side	Bottom line
Operator receives:	fixed cost	subsidy and revenue
Authority receives:	revenue and service	service only
Fares:	set by authority	only maximum fare set
Risks taken:	by authority	by operator (includes risk of competition)
Revenue collection:	monitored by authority	incentive for operator to maximise revenue

There is a Department of Transport Code of Practice on tendering which suggests that authorities might combine both the above types of tender into a hybrid "revenue guarantee agreement". This would be a bottom line tender under which the risk to the operators would be mitigated by guaranteeing a minimum revenue. The quid pro quo would be a maximum revenue above which the authority could recoup subsidy pro rata. This has the disadvantage of reducing the incentive to operators to exceed the maximum revenue figure as to do so would, for them, be partially self defeating.

Authorities are recommended by the Code of Practice to issue general invitations to tender by whatever means they consider will best bring these to the attention of potential operators. They may advertise their intention to let tenders and invite interested persons to register with them to receive details of these. Whilst only holders of O licences (and Community Bus Permits) may actually be awarded contracts, any person may register to receive tender documents; there can be no pre-qualification.

It is suggested that four weeks is a reasonable period to allow operators to submit tenders. After the tenders are received and opened, the authority has to decide which, if any, to accept. In doing so they must have regard *solely* to what they consider to be the most efficient and economic use of their funds. However, whilst best value for money is the paramount criterion, this does not mean automatic acceptance of the lowest tender, since authorities must also consider related expenditure on other services in the area, including Local Education Authorities' services and any other relevant matter.

A significant relevant matter might be the vehicle specification. For example, a minibus with high narrow gangways and little luggage storage space might be deemed inappropriate on a route on which a lot of shoppers or old people travel. The authority may also wish to inspect, or arrange to have inspected, the operator's vehicle, to assure themselves that it is safe and reliable. Account may also be taken of the operator's previous record of running registered local services.

After a tender is let, the authority has a further duty to publish certain statutory information. This includes:

(a)   the name of the successful tenderer;
(b)   the amount of the successful tender;
(c)   the number of tenders received;
(d)   the highest and lowest tenders.

Authorities may make acceptance of an operator's tender conditional on compliance with specific clauses in the tender document, such as the acceptance of school passes, concessionary fares or pre-purchased tickets, or meeting strict vehicle specifications, so long as such clauses cannot be construed as inhibiting competition. *Break clauses* are often inserted in contracts to cover both operator default or changes of circumstances, such as the registration of a competing commercial service.

Sometimes an authority may need to make an emergency agreement with an operator to plug a gap in service which has arisen unexpectedly. Perhaps a small operator has died or is ill, a vehicle has been destroyed by fire, or a new public transport requirement has suddenly cropped up. The service must however be put out to tender as soon as possible thereafter and the emergency agreement terminated not more than three months after the tender submission date.

Where an authority receives no tender at all, it is then free to negotiate an agreement with an operator of its choice.

De minimis agreements

Authorities are also given a certain amount of freedom to negotiate relatively insignificant service subsidy agreements without the need to go out to tender. This is known as the "de minimis provision" and covers agreements for an annual service subsidy under £4000 providing the operator does not receive more than £20,000 from any one tendering authority.

Of interest to minibus operators is the provision which allows existing service subsidies to Post Bus and Community Bus services to continue until 4.1.91 providing these were negotiated before 5.1.86.

Tendering is one way of "getting in on the act" of running a registered local bus service and since most tenders are for services which are clearly uneconomic when provided by conventional buses, minibus operators who often have considerably lower operating costs than their local large bus company, are well placed to win these.

Concessionary fares schemes

The Transport Act 1985 continued, with important modifications, the powers of local authorities, including, in Metropolitan Counties, Passenger Transport Authorities, to provide travel concession schemes.

Operators of eligible services on which concessions may be provided (ie registered local services attracting Fuel Tax Rebate) have a right to participate in schemes and indeed authorities may compel such participation.

Travel concessions may apply to:

(a) men of 65 and over and women of 60 and over;

(b) blind persons and disabled persons whose mobility is seriously impaired;

(c) children under 17 and those aged 17–19 in full time education;

(d) other classes of persons specified by order of the Secretary of State for Transport.

The principle behind reimbursement schemes is that authorities will have an obligation (but not a duty) to ensure that operators are *no better off nor any worse off* financially as a result of participating in their schemes. Arrangements are intended to be formulated to meet this objective since this is what the Secretary of State will have regard to in considering any applications to cancel or vary any participation notice.

The method of calculating the reimbursement of operators is based on loss of income sustained (LOIS) and is essentially the modified "revenue foregone" formula devised by the Chartered Institute of Public Finance and Accounts.

Since authorities may make concessions on some non-commercial routes by means of payments contained within the service subsidy agreement, a Code of Practice on Concessionary Fares Schemes has been drawn up by the Department of Transport which disallows simultaneous payment for concessionary travel on the route by means of reimbursement under a general scheme.

Operators would in any case need to know their take from the general scheme to be in a position to tender! Cases where "scheme" and "service subsidy" concessions become simultaneously available on a route could arise, for example, where a County Council provides child concessions on certain services under a service subsidy agreement and a District Council scheme provides child concessions under a general scheme to which the regulations apply.

Operators can only have an entitlement to an additional payment under a scheme where the concession is already funded under a service subsidy agreement in the event of the reimbursement under the scheme being greater than that under the subsidy agreement. In this case, the code suggests, there would be an entitlement to a net reimbursement to cover the difference.

Contracts for implementing schemes (whether voluntary or compulsory) should specify the:

(a) passes to be recognised;
(b) method of determining payment;
(c) information required from the operator;
(d) manner of making payments.

These arrangements should be those published by an authority in its scheme (unless they have been modified by the Secretary of State as a result of an operator's successful appeal against the scheme).

Reimbursement arrangements should be the subject of discussions between operators and the authority. Whilst token based schemes will provide information as to the number of concessionary journeys actually made, so far as pass based schemes are concerned, the code suggests three possibilities:

(a) Automatic recording of concessionary fares (for example by electronic ticketing).
(b) Sample surveys by the authority.
(c) Pooling on a patronage, revenue or mileage basis.

The basis on which re-imbursement is calculated is as follows. The amount of re-imbursement should equal:

(a) revenue which would have been received (calculated having regard to any additional fares generated – using a common generation factor) plus
(b) additional costs (for example the cost of any extra capacity required on the service to carry concessionary passengers and of any additional administration necessary) minus
(c) reductions in costs (for example where peak loadings are reduced by off peak concessions).

Payment periods must not be less frequent than once every three months, and interim payments of not less than 85% of the estimated amount due should be made at the mid point of each period, making any subsequently determined balancing payment not more than three months from the end of the period (six months in the case of the first six months of a newly established scheme).

Authorities may however withhold payments to operators who do not supply information in reasonable time.

They must adopt (and publish if they wish to use their powers of compulsion) standard methods of reimbursement. Details of any changes must also be published as these could give rise to a review of the status of any participation notices in effect at the time.

The Travel Concession Schemes Regulations (1986) also oblige authorities to take into account any operator's data which can be shown to be more accurate than the data used in the standard method and to adjust payments if the information on which they are based can be shown to be inaccurate in any way. Since many urban minibus schemes use electronic ticketing it is essential that drivers record concessionary fares or, where the concession is free travel, such journeys.

Standard methods of calculation of payment may be replaced by an agreement between the parties in the case of certain exempt small scale operations so long as doing so does not allow the authority thereby to discriminate in favour of one major operator at the expense of another. Small scale operations exempt from the requirement to supply data are those:

(a)   using vehicles with less than eight seats or
(b)   operating less than 100,000 miles within the scheme;
(c)   operating a service within the first three months of entrance to the scheme.

Some of the above are possible exemptions in the case of newly introduced minibus schemes.

Standard schemes might be drafted to allow for changes in some factors (for example, the price of a concessionary fare where fares have risen generally) to be made without thereby entailing a change in the scheme as a whole, since this would affect the status of participation notices.

Authorities in any case must review their schemes at least annually and publish details of any changes. Another regulation of possible use to minibus operators allows for some differentiation within the scheme between different operating zones and vehicle types.

Calculations of the fare values which would have been paid were the concession not made should take account of any discounts (such as low off peak fares) and be made by reference to either:

(a)   the fares normally paid (data can be derived from electronic ticketing or tokens) or
(b)   average fares paid on a service or group of services or
(c)   averages of all fares paid to all operators in a scheme where a pool based payment system is used.

Operators must be prepared to support any claims for additional costs associated with participation such as provision of extra capacity or those administrative costs of the scheme which fall on them (like the cost of data collection and preparation).

Authorities must treat data supplied by an operator as confidential unless the operator agrees otherwise.

Operators cannot be required to divulge:

(a)   the cost of providing a service;
(b)   their operating turnover;

(c) their annual profit or loss;
but may be required to provide data on
(a) patronage or ridership on the service;
(b) revenue derived from concessionary fares.
If the data is requested in a disaggregate form because the scheme distinguishes between different types of operation, it must not be required in a form capable of identifying different operators' individual services, unless the operators themselves volunteer to do so.

Authorities may make reimbursement conditional upon operators supporting their information with a certificate of accuracy issued by a responsible person; either a member of the Institute of Chartered Accountants or the Chartered Association of Certified Accountants.

Information may not be requested more frequently than every 28 days in the case of patronage data and every three months in the case of revenue data.

Authorities have a right to survey passengers travelling at concessionary fares on an operator's services and to obtain other information regarding the number of concessionary passengers and the fares they pay, and may install and require operators to use equipment designed for this purpose, (eg electronic ticket issuing machines or pass readers).

The code suggests authorities should preferably reach agreement about the use of such equipment by operators, perhaps on a pool basis. However, infrastructure grants may be claimed under the provisions of the Transport Act 1968 to cover the capital cost of the equipment subject to its being freely available to all operators so as not to inhibit competition. The DTp is sponsoring the establishment of a British Standard for magnetically encoded travel cards.

Authorities may require operators to supply details of fares and service changes within 7 days of their taking effect. Up to 42 days' notice of withdrawal from voluntary participation in a scheme may be required by an authority and failure to supply concessions in this period could result in a conviction.

Authorities responsible for administering a scheme may employ agents to act on their behalf but these may not be PSV O licence holders. However operators may be employed as pass or ticket issuing agents (but not in relation to reimbursement).

Operators can be required to display on their vehicles a notice indicating the availability of concessions and to accept passes and tokens issued by or for the authority. Operators may require that passengers claiming concessionary travel can demonstrate their entitlement. No provisions in any scheme may require operators to operate their services any differently than they would do so if they were not participating.

The regulations provide for the content of notices and the manner in which they can be served. The particulars in schedule 1 of the regulations, identifying the operator, authority and service(s) are common to all the following.

Schedule	Given by	Given to	Content
2	authority	operator	intention to modify reimbursement
3	authority	operator	participation notice
4	authority	operator	variation notice
5	operator	Secretary of State	seeking cancellation/variation of schedule 3

There are two grounds for a schedule 5 application, namely:
   (a)   that participation is inappropriate in respect of a particular service because either,
      (i)   it does not serve local transport needs, even though "eligible" (an example would be a premium service such as an airport link) or
      (ii)   the standard repayment calculation is inappropriate;
   (b)   that reimbursement arrangements are in general inappropriate to all operators required to participate.

Copies of schedule 5 notices must be sent to the authority, giving the date of application or intended application to the Secretary of State at least seven days before this date. They may be delivered by hand, recorded delivery or registered post.

Authorities must permit entry to schemes but may control entry by prescribing entry dates not more than three months apart and requiring operators to give at least 28 days' notice of their intention to participate from that date. The maximum duration of a compulsory notice will be three years. They can be effective 28 days after being served.

They must also give at least 28 days' notice of a variation to a scheme and allow time for operators to indicate their intention to carry on participating or to withdraw. Since a further 28 days would be required for a fresh participation notice to become effective, in practice authorities will need to give at least 56 days' notice of variation to ensure continuity of concessions.

Operators and authorities are required to supply to the Secretary of State, and to copy to each other, written statements of their position in relation to cancellation or variation applications. Deadlines may be set by the Secretary of State and if these are not met the application will fail.

The code points out that unlike applications under (a) above, which could result merely in the release of the operator from his or her obligation to participate, applications under (b) made on the grounds of inappropriateness of the scheme to all operators would have wider implications and could result in the Secretary of State having to indicate to an authority the ways in which he or she thinks the scheme is at fault. It would then almost certainly be necessary for the authority to make general changes in the scheme.

Schedule 5 is the basis of the operator's case and the regulations provide for the authority to respond within 28 days (unless an extension of time is allowed by the Secretary of State). He or she may, for example, ask either party for further clarification of their statements. At least 14 days must be allowed for this unless both parties agree otherwise. As above, statements must be copied by each party to the other. These may contain factual comment and supporting material.

The Secretary of State may decide to conduct a hearing in some (not all) cases. He or she must give at least 14 days' notice of this. Both parties may be represented or present their own cases. They may call and cross examine witnesses. Documentary and "hearsay" evidence is admissible. If an authority wishes to quote information relating to another operator it must obtain his or her consent.

A nominee may be appointed by the Secretary of State to act on his or her behalf. His or her decision will be promulgated in writing and communicated to both parties. It will include a brief explanation of the grounds on which it has been made. Summaries of these decisions, to be published by the DTp, will eventually give a clear indication of how the regulations are being operated.

Concessionary fares support is an important source of revenue and minibus operators who disregard the opportunity to participate in an authority's scheme disadvantage themselves in relation to their competitors who are participating. They also render themselves liable to being served with a compulsory participation notice. Some Community Transport operators offer their clients concessions within a county-wide scheme.

Nor should it be forgotten that a significant proportion of concessionary riders are children, who will be the adult fare paying passengers of tomorrow. It is shortsighted not to cultivate this market.

Off-bus ticket sales

Before deregulation many PTEs and Shire County transport co-ordinators ran pre-paid ticketing schemes. These were in the form of straightforward commercial marketing ploys to encourage maximum use of their supported network, especially at off-peak times.

The range of pre-paid tickets was wide, covering weekly and monthly season tickets, "clippercards" for various fares (peak, off-peak and concessionary) sold at a discount and cancelled on the vehicle and zone tickets giving unlimited travel within and between nominated travel zones. Many of these schemes became early casualties of deregulation.

The reason for this was not hard to see. Operators saw less commercial sense in promoting travel throughout a network if some of the services on that network were operated by their competitors.

However, the buses White Paper, which introduced deregulation, claimed that it would be in "operators' own commercial interests" to continue these or similar arrangements since passengers would clearly still require to make journeys across an area, perhaps involving a change of vehicle and operator and would find the off-bus pre-purchase of area-wide tickets attractive. In other words, continuance of the system might be expected to retain and possibly even generate traffic for all operators.

Critics of deregulation saw off-bus ticketing as an early casualty. The reality is that in some areas the PTE or Shire County has formed operator panels to determine the details of the scheme to which the members subscribe. In Tyne and Wear the panel has been re-constituted as a limited company owned by the operators.

The price and availability of tickets, any discounts and the selling outlets, must be agreed. The scheme has to be open to all operators who wish to participate and even then needs to be made the subject of a registered commercial agreement with the OFT to ensure that it does not inhibit competition (see Chapter 5).

Despite good intentions, there are whole areas today which had off-bus pre-paid ticketing before deregulation but do not now and there are signs of strain in some operators' panels where individual operators, who perhaps feel that for them the disadvantages of the scheme could outweigh its advantages, are tempted to break ranks, or where the panel has whittled down the scheme to a shadow of its original import.

For minibus operators the question must be faced. Is it better to participate in the scheme or to try and build up a brand loyalty to their own services? Most passengers, especially in inclement weather, catch the first bus to come along which is going their way. Issuing return tickets for use on the minibus service only might capture some traffic but it is the author's view that where a service shares a road with other operators, interavailability of a "third party" ticket (in other words sold on behalf of the panel rather than the operator) can actually generate considerable additional traffic.

If the minibus operator decides to break ranks with the panel and not accept all or some of the pre-paid tickets, he or she runs the risk of the major operator retaliating by devising a pre-sold ticketing system for his or her own passengers which will not be valid on the competitors' minibuses (but will be valid on his or her own mini-buses!). This actually happened in 1987 in one large Passenger Transport Area.

What the minibus operators need to ensure is that the rules for sharing the revenue from off-bus ticketing are fair to them. Often these are similar to the rules for sharing the concessionary fare pool and based on the Concessionary Fare Code of Practice, which is quite even handed as between conventional bus operators and minibus operators and usually based on an independent sample of ridership.

Under such a regime the minibus operator has everything to gain and little to lose by participating in an off bus pre-paid ticketing system. It is worth remembering also that revenue from pre-paid tickets is "up front", that is, paid before the journey is made and, providing the pooling and sharing arrangements are efficient, can only help the minibus operator's cash flow.

CHAPTER 7 *Marketing*

Urban minibus conversions epitomise the new post deregulation market philosophy. They are demand led, not product led like the conventional licensed stage carriage services they replace. Most could be used by any student as an excellent case study supporting the theory of marketing.

Marketing, the theoreticians tell us, is simply the identification and satisfaction of demand. To do this, various steps must be taken.

First, demand must be measured. This involves market research, not just into the journeys which passengers wish to make in terms of origin, destination and time (although these are crucial factors) but also into questions like the value which passengers place on speed, comfort, frequency, reliability, safety, etc.

The next step is to design a service to meet the demand which has been identified. Chapter 3 on minibus operation contains helpful advice in this context.

The service must then be promoted and operated, and after that its performance must be monitored. Chapter 6 suggests how electronic ticketing systems can help at this stage. It is important also to monitor how any competitor is responding. Any adjustments suggested by the results of this monitoring must then be made, either within the 42 days registration period, or sooner if one of the loopholes in the registration regulations can be used (see Chapter 5).

Marketing is not just these four steps; it is a continuous and ongoing activity. Ideally the marketing philosophy should permeate the whole undertaking, not just remain the concern of a specialised marketing department. All staff, especially drivers, should be made to feel part of the exercise. They are closest to the market and their observations and suggestions are ignored at the operator's peril.

The marketing mix

Textbooks talk of the four Ps — product, price, promotion and place.

Chapters 3 and 6 respectively have dealt with the first two of these but the others are also of paramount importance.

Operators should be aware that not every place is automatically the right one in which to apply the "minibus solution". The Jack Report (see Chapter 1) observed that minibuses are not the universal panacea for rural transport. Nor are they the most suitable vehicles for extremely heavily loaded city routes, for which double-deck buses were designed and are still best (although articulated vehicles are also excellent movers of large loads). Heavy commuter flows, school services to and from large comprehensive schools and football fans are just a few examples of situations for which the minibus is not suitable.

Urban minibus schemes are ideally suited to what has become known as *medium level* demand; that is, something halfway between a busy commuter route and a rural community bus service. Although demand on any service is bound to peak at rush hours, minibus services thrive where it is also continuous and spontaneous.

Traffic in suburban areas tends to be continuous throughout the day with school, shopping, work, social and business journeys, and some of these are also spontaneous, as when housewives shop further afield than normal, or visit friends, and when children make additional trips in the evenings, at the weekend and in holiday times. It is from these sorts of trips that the generated traffic which is characteristic of minibus conversions is known to come. The reason is primarily the convenience and frequency of the service.

The market for a public passenger transport service is only different to the market for most products in that the service is perishable (seat miles, once provided, if not "bought" by passengers cannot be resold). Most providers of products with a perishable market (eg newspapers) recognise that the market is segmented. In other words, there are niches in the market where their product sells well. It would be as pointless to promote *The Times* at the Durham Miners' Gala as to try and sell *The Guardian* at the Conservative Party Conference.

Minibuses, no less than Sock Shop, Tie Rack, Next or Body Shop, cater for a niche market and operators are discovering that their niche, at the moment, is the high frequency suburb-town urban minibus service. In the case of some smaller towns it is the entire town service network.

Only by continuous research and monitoring can they be sure that they are still in the right market. Today's niche can become tomorrow's grave.

Market research

Many operators have done some quite extensive market research into minibus operation. The National Bus Company, before it was wound up, had developed MAP (the Market Analysis Project) which was widely recognised as one of the most sophisticated and successful public transport market research models of its kind and it is certain that MAP data was used as the basis for some of the original experiments.

Midland Red (North) conducted a useful attitudinal survey on bus users' preferences, with the following interesting result:

85% preferred minibuses;

11% no preference;

4% did not prefer minibuses.

When an attempt was made to establish the reasons for the high preference of minibuses, these results were obtained:

62% frequency;
42% hail and ride;
27% convenience;
15% speed.

Passenger ratings, on a scale one (poor) to ten (excellent) were elicited for minibuses vis a vis the old conventional bus service they had replaced.

	Minibus	Old service
Frequency	9.4	6.9
Speed	8.9	7.9
Comfort	7.8	7.1
Cleanliness	9.1	6.5

The last rating perhaps reflected the newness of the vehicles but it is also noticeable that minibuses attract very little vandalism, probably because of the more intimate driver-passenger relationship and the closer driver supervision which their small size makes possible.

The comfort ratings for minibuses were surprising but passenger ratings of the vehicle and its characteristics give some idea of the areas to which operators will need to pay more attention in future:

vehicle entrance/exit   7.4
luggage provision   5.1
warmth/ventilation   8.1
smoothness of ride   7.8
friendliness of:
   drivers   9.6
   passengers   8.6

The last two ratings, together wtih the 42% preference for hail and ride operations, give the clue to another traffic generation factor. Old people and single women, especially at night, who might feel vulnerable or threatened at bus stops or on the top deck or even in the saloon of a conventional bus, feel confident to undertake a journey by minibus which they would not otherwise have made.

The most consistent complaints about minibuses concern the difficulty of access/egress with shopping, trolleys and luggage, the narrow gangways and the lack of luggage space. The new generation of PSV specification mini/midibuses is addressing all these problems.

There is clearly scope for more market research into minibus passenger preferences but one fact on which most operators are agreed is that the level of passenger complaints reduces when minibuses are introduced.

Promotion

"Sell the benefits, not the product" is advice as old as the oldest marketing textbook. It is nonetheless sound advice. Minibus services have significant benefits to their users, as well as, it must be admitted, some drawbacks.

It is often claimed that the minibus' ability to penetrate difficult routes denied to conventional vehicles enables them to capture additional traffic. Operators have found that whilst a moderate degree of "fantail and loop" operation along branching routes at outer trip ends is acceptable, what passengers value most is fast transit to the town centre along the main "desire lines". In most cases these are the main radial routes.

Cross town routes with layover at the outer terminuses are also preferred by some operators to town centre stands, especially as these allow short journeys to be made within the downtown area. Instant start up of the service is then possible by inserting vehicles into the route simultaneously at different points.

Routes generally, it has been found, should not exceed three or four miles using the present generation of vehicles based on commercial chassis. Beyond that a more comfortable vehicle is needed. Possibly the next generation of "PSV specification" minibuses and more robust midibuses might fill another marketing slot, the four to six mile route?

Standing on minibuses with narrow gangways whilst having to allow passengers to squeeze past is marginally less pleasant than on a conventional bus and routes and frequencies should be planned to avoid this over any significant distance at all but the busiest times. Some passengers also report mild claustrophobia in a crowded minibus with the maximum number of standing passengers.

Running times as much as 30% better than the buses they replace are often possible using minibuses and this itself is a major attraction. The TRRL has found that total costs are actually more sensitive to variations in round trip running times than to any other factor, including labour and vehicle costs.

There is no doubt by now that high frequency minibus operation is attractive to passengers. The main reason for this seems to be "perceived continuity – no waiting" (already known as the PCNW factor). This is especially true in winter and in rain when research has shown that perceived waiting time is often double the actual waiting time.

Promoting a new or existing minibus service should stress all these benefits. Press releases to do this should be prepared by competent staff, or professional copywriters should be employed. Press announcements and advertisements must precede new services and changes. Free circulation papers can be used to make sure that every household receives a copy of the timetable, either as part of an advertisement in the paper, or as an insert. Local radio is also useful. Newly recruited drivers to drop leaflets through letterboxes. This helps familiarise them with "their" area.

It is worthwhile considering giving free travel on the first day of the service, possibly accompanied by some promotional material such as children's hats or balloons featuring the service brand name. The exercise can be billed as a fun day when passengers meet "their" minibus and drivers.

Branding, in fact, is a powerful promotional tool. Many of the original NBC minibus networks were given brand names which emphasised some of the benefits such as quicker and more frequent journeys, small friendly vehicles (the so called diminutive ploy) and innovation. Examples include:

Buzzibus	Mini Link	Nipper
Dart	Hopper	City Line

Ribble Motors of Preston, an ex NBC subsidiary, who acquired United Transport International's minibuses, kept the brand names of Buzzy Bee and Zippy. Greater Manchester Buses emphasise the quality of their service with the name Little Gem.

Some undertakings attempt to link their own name to their minibuses, for example, Midland Fox's Fox Cubs and Badgerline's Baby Badger. Others attempt to achieve a regional identity by using a brand name linked to the town, thus ReddiLink in Redditch.

Advertising slogans such as "Fast, Frequent, Friendly" can be displayed on minibuses and hoardings.

Bus stop displays are an important promotional element and need to be both informative and attractive. Operators will do well to make sure that details of their services are displayed in local libraries, post offices and local authority offices.

It is not just urban minibus services which require promotion, of course. Other minibus uses have to be announced to their intended clientele. Thus Community Transport operators spend much time and effort in extending their client base by promoting their services through welfare organisations, at day centres, libraries, social service offices and via the trade associations which look after the interests of proprietors of rest homes.

Marketing a rural Community Bus service by comparison may be relatively simple, involving little more than plugging into the village grapevine – the pub, post office, village shop, church, WVS and primary school; but it has to be done, nonetheless.

Where a minibus operator wishes to encourage the private hire of his or her vehicles off peak and at weekends, an appropriate marketing exercise amongst pubs, clubs, churches, schools, etc must be undertaken. The minibus is an ideal vehicle for certain niches of the private hire market; for example the pub darts team, which is just too small for a conventional coach.

Mr Bob Montgomery, the Manager of United Transport International's extensive Buzzy Bee minibus network in South Manchester, talking about promoting a new service, remarked "every problem is an opportunity". Whilst every promotion has an element of razzamatazz, its importance should not be underestimated.

Customer care

It is claimed that minibuses are user friendly. Obviously the marketing role of the driver-salesperson is crucial and staff selection and training is therefore paramount. The environment of a bus with 25 or less seats is "intimate" and the driver can observe every passenger. There is little vandalism and next to no fare evasion.

However, transport services are highly visible to their public. It is difficult if not impossible to disguise malfunctions in the service. The late running or absence of a minibus is self evident because there is usually no immediate substitute (apart from the undesirable, from the operator's point of view, substitute of a competitor's service). Bus services are also, in economic terms, perishable – in other words, once provided, if not used, they cannot, like other consumer products, be stored. A seat/mile unsold is a seat mile lost. This is why it is so important to ensure that staff do all in their power to prevent "gaps" in the service.

Drivers are the ambassadors of their undertaking and it is of paramount importance therefore that they are trained to understand their passengers' perceptions of the service and to help them with their difficulties. They are exposed to their passengers like the actors on a stage and their behaviour reflects on their employer.

When passengers board a vehicle it is not usually with the express purpose of having a nice ride but because they want to arrive at a destination in safety and on time. The nice ride is a bonus.

The price of arriving safely and on time is the fare, which the driver must charge the passenger. Psychologists have found that although passengers do not perceive the payment of a fare as distressing, it is precisely that – a "distress purchase" in marketing jargon. In other words it does not give the same immediate pleasure as, for example, the purchase of an ice cream or a pint of beer but it relieves them of the cash which they would rather have spent on beer or ice cream.

Interestingly, passengers do not perceive off-the-bus sales in the same light, which is one good reason for operators promoting these; they are good for passenger relations.

Not surprisingly, then, many driver/passenger confrontations arise at the farebox (or when fare payment is being checked by an inspector).

Understanding passengers

To avoid needless confrontations drivers need to be able to understand their passengers. Many passengers are insecure but try to hide this because no one likes to look foolish in public. The insecurity can arise in many ways:

  (a) they may not know the fare to their destination and are afraid to ask the driver because he or she looks unfriendly;

(b)   they may be afraid of being late for an appointment or a connection;

(c)   they may be afraid of boarding the wrong vehicle and going astray;

(d)   they may be having difficulty disentangling complex information on signs, bus stop display boards or timetables (services are changing so rapidly after deregulation that it is easy to sympathise with confused passengers – many drivers are equally confused);

(e)   they may have children or elderly persons "in tow";

(f)   they may be young, elderly or disabled themselves;

(g)   bus stations, airports and railway terminals are confusing places, scenes of hectic activity, and passengers can easily become confused and insecure.

Good passenger care simply involves recognising passenger anxiety, making allowances for irrational passenger behaviour and trying to be helpful and reassuring.

In even the best run service, things will go wrong, and there is little point in staff pretending everything is fine when passengers can see that it is not. Complaints will always arise, both justified and not, but the way in which these are handled can in itself become good customer care and enhance the undertaking's image. A problem can be turned into an opportunity.

Many complaints are genuine but simply arise out of a misunderstanding or misinformation and can be disposed of on the spot. Others require more careful handling.

Most, but not all, people find it difficult to complain. If passengers feel that they have a genuine complaint, they want to be reassured that it will be taken seriously. So drivers should always acknowledge complaints. Obviously, if they can deal with it they should do so but if not, they should offer to pass it on to the person who can deal with it, or give the passengers details of how they can make the complaint formally if they do not wish the driver to do so.

Most passengers will be happy for drivers to take up their complaints for them if they feel that the drivers can be trusted to do so. Of course it goes without saying that the complaint must then be passed on, so it is a good idea to get a name and address or telephone number so that passengers can be informed of the outcome of their complaints.

Competition

Established operators of conventional bus services are extremely vulnerable to competition from minibuses, especially since deregulation. This is said to apply to any urban operator on any route with a frequency of ten minutes or more. Bearing in mind that if a minibus service with a frequency of less than ten minutes is registered there is no need to submit a timetable with the registration, the scope for intensive competition seems limitless.

It is known that large bus operators often tend to exaggerate the size of their peak hour commitment when justifying their double-deck fleets. Since deregulation many school services have been included in hybrid tendered services available to all the travelling public, including school children, thus syphoning off much schools traffic and flattening the operator's peak. Despite this, the size of the established operators' large vehicles which they keep for this peak demand will still dictate a low off peak frequency – hence their vulnerability.

From a marketing point of view a sensitively converted high frequency minibus scheme can make the established operator's position almost impregnable. This must be one reason why NBC converted so many routes prior to deregulation.

The Transport Act 1985, in bringing bus services within the ambit of competition law and in giving Traffic Commissioners powers to take action against operators who do not run their services as registered or who intentionally interfere with another operator's registered service, attempts to make sure that competition is engaged in fairly.

It is always counter productive for operators or drivers to engage in a war with their competitors. Although retribution is, by the nature of this legislation, regrettably slow, it is nonetheless sure.

The generation factor

According to the TRRL, there is no general rule concerning ridership growth on minibus conversion schemes. However, they note that growth has been particularly marked from high income areas, although they qualify this by observing that such growth was often from a very low base, such as a very poor and infrequent conventional bus service.

It is this growth – their by now well known ability to generate additional traffic, often in quite staggering amounts – which is considered to be the major attraction of high frequency minibus schemes to operators.

Very few schemes report less than 40% traffic generation and in some of the longer running schemes it is reported to be over 100%! Sometimes, but not always, this is a reflection on the dreadful pre-minibus level of service.

Usually however, operators report that the generation of traffic is largely in the off peak between 09.30 and 16.00 hours. This is the profitable part of minibus operation and traffic can build up to 70% or 80% of peak traffic. During this period 65% of passengers are female. Generation of OAP traffic has in the main proved disappointing.

Routes with loading of 320–400 passengers per minibus per day can be extremely profitable and this scale of operation is by no means unusual. Costs as low as 60p per mile (at 1986 prices) have been reported on some intensive operations and revenue often exceeds costs by over 25%.

There is some evidence in a paper given by the General Manager of Midland Red (North), Mr Ian Mitchell, to the 1986 Summer Conference of the Association of Transport Co-ordinating Officers that the generation factor is a function of the frequency increase. He gave the following figures:

Town	Frequency increase	% Passenger growth
A	×3	80
B	×2	40
C	×5	100

Some operators are already voicing an opinion that on some converted routes traffic generation might be so good that conventional buses can be reintroduced.

Publicity

Most urban minibus schemes have been launched amidst intense publicity. Publicity is an essential ingredient of any promotion. Passengers need information and obtain this in person and by phone from enquiry points at the undertaking's offices, in bus stations and possibly at centrally located kiosks, off-bus ticket sales points and, of course, on the vehicle.

Staff responsible for publicity, and this includes drivers, inspectors and enquiry clerks, must be trained in good customer care practices and possess adequate product knowledge of the undertaking's services to be able to help enquirers.

The argument as to whether operators should stock and dispense their competitors' publicity is really no different from the argument rehearsed in Chapter 6 over whether to participate in off-bus ticketing schemes. On balance it will be in the commercial interests of all operators to co-operate in selling each other's services.

For the staff of an operator to inform an intending passenger that there is no Sunday service on that undertaking's route where a competitor has won a tender for Sunday workings will hardly endear the operator to the passenger when he or she discovers the truth.

One aspect of publicity is publications, ie the actual printed material which is sold or more usually given away to intending passengers. The design of this, especially promotional handbills, must be sufficiently professional to enhance rather than detract from the minibus operator's reputation.

With the instability of services which came with deregulation and because operators wish to feel free to alter timings with the minimum of administrative inconvenience possible to respond to competition, the trend today is away from area-wide timetable booklets towards individual service timetable leaflets.

Timetables

The timetable is to the minibus operator what the shop window is to the retailer. It should be informative and attractive and give a point of reference (preferably a telephone or even answerphone number) where the passenger can receive up-to-date information.

The peculiarities of the registration regulations, discussed in Chapter 5, mean that it is not necessary to give actual timings where the frequency of a service is every ten minutes or less. However, it is desireable to do so, even if the timetable only says 7.05am and every $7\frac{1}{2}$ minutes until 9.35am, then every 10 minutes until . . ." etc.

Even high frequency services tend to have a lower frequency at night and on Sundays, and a timetable which lurches between "every five minutes" and 7.30pm and "every 15 minutes" looks untidy and inconsistent.

There is debate about whether to use the 24 hour clock or am/pm timings. This is really for the operator to decide in the light of such factors as the proportion of OAPs (who tend to dislike the 24 hour clock) who are likely to use a service. Where am/pm timings are used, they can usefully be distinguished by different type faces.

Most timetables have the timing points arranged down a column at the left of the page and individual journey times in columns to the right of these. However, for short routes with few timing points, an attractive timetable can be presented with timing points at the head of the page and timings in rows below these.

A schematic map showing the route of the minibus is appreciated by passengers unfamiliar with the area, as is a faretable if this is not too complicated and there is room to present it without the leaflet becoming cluttered.

Although the essence of an urban minibus conversion is the PCNW factor this should not excuse operators from the need to prepare timetables. Passengers want to be reassured that their reliable minibus service will be along when they need it and this may be 7am, 11.30pm or Sunday night. The timetable will ensure that when it is there they catch *it* and not a taxi.

CHAPTER 8 *The Future and Other "Mini Matters"*

A number of question marks hang over the minibus revolution. Does it, as has already been suggested by its detractors, contain the seeds of its own destruction? Is it the victim of its own success and will friendly frequent minibuses turn into impersonal infrequent midibuses? Will minibuses last long enough to justify their capital expenditure and will there be a secondhand market for them at the end of their local service life?

Diagnosis of the problem – the decline of conventional urban bus services, and one answer – minibuses, was comparatively easy compared to any attempted prognosis of the course which "minibus fever" might run.

Vehicle life and replacement policy

Already, in the short three or four years since the start of the minibus revolution there have been surprises. Operators of the first generation of high frequency urban minibuses are expressing pleasant surprise at how well these have stood up to the rigours of operation.

There were some early problems with components like brake linings and transmissions. However, bus engineers are resourceful folk and solutions in the form of disc brakes, retarders and automatic transmissions were quickly found. The next generation of integral and PSV-specific minibuses and midibuses (see Chapter 4) incorporated these solutions into their design.

It will be interesting to monitor operators' replacement policy in the future. For the moment it is only possible to guess at them. Experience suggests that the more heavily engineered chassis will increasingly come to be chosen and that larger minibuses or even midibuses will be specified.

Probably minibuses like the Talbot Express, the CVE Omni and the Metrorider will find increasing favour with operators as they are designed as buses and are not adaptations of commercial vehicles. They tackle some of the more common passenger criticisms of minibuses (see Chapter 7).

Replacement policy is dictated to some extent by the market for secondhand vehicles. Where this is bouyant and operators can dispose of their vehicles for a good price they are more inclined to replace them.

With over 80,000 minibuses in use at the moment, of which approximately 8000 (or 10%) are in use as PSVs, there would seem on the face of it to be no problem of the secondhand market drying up. However, there is a cloud on the horizon in the shape of the Eurolicence proposal for a unitary ordinary/vocational licence.

Ironically, if the United Kingdom were to obtain a derogation from the need for a passenger carrying vehicle licence for drivers of vehicles with 9–16 seats, this will make the disposal of minibuses with more than 16 seats to voluntary organisations, schools, clubs and charities that much more difficult.

The secondhand minibus market will become segmented between minibuses (employing the strict legal definition) with 16 or less seats and buses with 17 or more seats and the market for the latter will be extremely "sticky".

How safe?

Fears that widespread use of minibuses would lower safety standards have not been born out by results. A survey by the TRRL in 1985 and 1986 showed the following casualty rates per million passenger kilometres.

Vehicle	Total casualties	Serious/fatal
Buses	19	
Minibuses	21	10
Cars	33	

These findings agree with the general impression amongst insurance companies, brokers and operators. Bearing in mind that 40% of all accidents to PSV passengers occur during boarding and alighting whilst the vehicle is stationary this is an impressive safety record for any industry.

It is however nothing to be complacent about, since DTp statistics show a marginal increase in the number of "failures before rectification" of PSVs submitted for annual test since deregulation. To counter that, under the Transport Act 1985 minibuses are now subject to roadside checks in the same way as buses always have been.

Technological advances

In common with all passenger vehicles, recent models display impressive technological advances over their predecessors. Under the bonnet electronic ignition and plug in points for electronic fault diagnosis are becoming standard. Disc brakes all round, automatic braking control, automatic transmission, retarders and air suspension are becoming more common. All of these are pushing prices up to nearer £1200 per seat than the old yardstick of £1000, but they are reducing maintenance costs and vehicle downtime.

A side effect of minibuses becoming "microchips on wheels" is the training of the staff who maintain them and the real skill shortage of fitters sufficiently up to date in their trade to work on these technologically advanced vehicles.

The minibus may also contain electronic ticket machines, electric tachographs, automatic vehicle guidance/location systems and sophisticated band three radios. The vehicle is climbing the same sophistication curve as the conventional bus climbed when it went from front engine rear loading buses (like the London Routemaster) to complex rear engine one person operated buses.

In some cases the labour saving costs of shedding a conductor were almost negated by the higher operating cost of the new generation bus. There may be a moral here for minibus operators, if only to observe the renaissance of conductors in some undertakings.

London services

London, like the provinces is to be deregulated. So much is provided for in the Transport Act 1985 and so much is promised by Government ministers. How and when is the question.

Already London Bus (the bus operating arm of London Regional Transport) has been restructured into manageable operating units. LRT is already a tendering authority, although service subsidy agreements won by tender come at present with an LRT Bus Operating Agreement which precludes competition on the route. It is said that LRT would like to be the registration authority for London when deregulation comes.

A few minibus services have been put out to tender and won already, in some cases by London Buses, in others by independent operators. The attempt by Associated Minibus Operators (AMOS) to franchise a minibus service in London has already been referred to in Chapter 5 and is considered in more depth below. Since AMOS's lack of success in achieving this, Shuttlebus, on appeal to the Secretary of State for Transport and against the advice of his inspector, secured a London Bus Agreement for a high frequency minibus operation based on Heathrow Airport (this was a conventional operation using employee drivers).

No one knows how London deregulation will go; the above are mere straws in the wind. What seems certain, however, is that there will be a place for minibus operators.

96 MINIBUS SERVICES

The case for franchising

The 1983 attempt, by Mr Anthony Shepherd, to form AMOS for the purpose of running, in agreement he hoped, with London Transport Executive, two high frequency cross London minibus services, did not, as has already been pointed out, succeed at the time.

When London Transport Executive refused to enter into such an agreement, AMOS appealed to the Secretary of State for Transport, who appointed as his inspector to hear the appeal, Vice Admiral Sir Stephen Berthon KCB.

The concept of franchising was central to the AMOS proposal. Over 350 Ford Transit Minibuses owned by AMOS were to be leased to their drivers (leasing associates) who would operate these under AMOS's control and whose earnings would be dependent upon the revenue from each vehicle.

The Secretary of State dismissed the AMOS appeal, giving as his reasons for doing so the findings of his inspector. When this decision was promulgated in June 1984 many busmen felt that it was the end of the road for franchising.

The inspector had not been convinced that AMOS's operating costs would be as low as it envisaged nor that the proposed management structure and code of operation was sufficiently credible to ensure a satisfactory and safe level of operation. He also criticised the lack of a firm policy on tachographs and commented that the parking of large numbers of vehicles when out of service would have an adverse effect on the environment.

It was submitted to the inspector that AMOS's proposal to hold the PSV O licence would lead to immediate illegal operation. This is not precisely the same thing as the reason given by the Secretary of State for dismissing the appeal, namely that "in order for the proposed service to be operated within the terms of the law the individual leasing associates would require London Bus Agreements and that any agreement granted to AMOS would not empower the provision by such leasing associates of the proposed service".

Franchising minibus operations is obviously an attractive proposition to a large bus operator, as it overcomes several problems at once; namely the initial capital cost (born by the franchisee under a loan or leasing agreement), the industrial relations problems associated with employing large numbers of minibus drivers and the difficulties of operator and driver licensing (which can be made to fall on the franchisee).

A close reading of the inspector's decision can actually lead to the conclusion that the franchising of minibus operations could be done legally, at least so far as operations outside London are concerned, for the following reasons.

(a) The position of a franchisee in respect of PSV O licensing has not been tested in the traffic courts.

(b) Any appeal against the refusal of a Traffic Commissioner to grant an O licence to a franchisor would now lie with the Transport Tribunal, which has already addressed itself to similar situations in the road haulage industry and reached surprisingly generous conclusions.

(c) In a deregulated environment (outside London) the question of refusal of operating consent by a PTE or County Council could not arise so individual leasing associates would not be required to make individual operating agreements.

(d) Traffic Commissioners are precluded from taking into account environmental matters when disposing of an application for a PSV O licence so the objection of unsightly parking, though real enough, would not be admissible.

It is useful to examine how the Traffic Commissioners and the Tribunal have dealt with non standard forms of operation up to now, as this should give some indication as to the possible outcome if another AMOS-type application were to come before a provincial Traffic Commissioner.

The crux of the problem lies in deciding whether an operator can use self employed drivers. The Public Passenger Vehicles Act 1981 defines the operator of a PSV as:

(i)   the driver, if he owns the vehicle; and

(ii) in any other case the person for whom the driver works (whether under a contract of employment or any other description of contract personally to do work).

This is similar, but more explicit, than the equivalent definition under goods vehicle operator licensing law (Transport Act 1968) which makes the operator "the driver, or the person whose servant or agent the driver is".

In one of the earliest cases to test this definition (*Readymix Concrete Ltd* v *Yorkshire Area Licensing Authority*) which went on appeal to the Queen's Bench Division in 1970 the court held that every owner driver who worked exclusively for Readymix, delivering concrete on vehicles supplied to them by the company, must hold an O licence.

However, in 1984 (*Kammac Trucking* v *NWLA*) the Transport Tribunal said:

It does not follow that just because an operator employs only self employed drivers to drive his vehicles that he is therefore an unfit person to hold an O licence nor does it follow that he will necessarily have inadequate financial resources to maintain them.

This was the first time that the Tribunal had given, however obliquely, its blessing to operators using self employed drivers. The test case, however, was undoubtedly *Gordon Wright Transport* v *Eastern Area LA* (Transport Tribunal 1985). The licensing authority (the term given by goods vehicle operators to the Traffic Commissioner) had interpreted the Transport Act 1968 to mean that there was no provision for an operator to have self employed drivers.

The expression "servant or agent" is in fact only used in Part VI of the Act which relates to drivers' hours but it does have relevance in Part V, since in s. 64 there is a requirement on the applicant for an O licence to satisfy the licensing authority that the hours regulations will be complied with.

On appeal from the licensing authority's refusal to grant the licence, the Transport Tribunal was referred to an earlier precedent in which the Queen's Bench Division Court had held that a driver, whilst he was driving, was "employed" by the person for whom he was driving, and another High Court case in which it had been held that an agency driver was to be treated as an employee driver by the hiring company.

In view of these conditions and applying the common law test of employment – whether there is power to hire and fire, not whether the driver was liable for tax and National Insurance contributions – the Tribunal decided that the self employed drivers of Mr Wright were in fact "employees" for O licensing purposes. Mr Wright, it transpired, had dismissed four drivers who would not comply with his "instructions".

The conclusion which can be drawn from the above is that any operator applying for a PSV O licence to operate a service using self employed drivers would probably be successful. Of course, until an operator tries this and is either granted the licence or goes on appeal to the Tribunal it cannot be known if this is the right conclusion.

Even if it is held that each driver must hold an O licence, this need not stop a determined franchisor from going ahead with a scheme. Although each driver would need to obtain a PSV National CPC, this could be a condition of awarding the franchise and, in view of the large number of trainees likely to be involved, the operator would find no shortage of training organisations prepared to negotiate a package deal.

Reference was made in Chapter 5 to the inspector's conclusions in the AMOS case, where he said "I believe that AMOS are justified in their view that there is a case for the introduction of a spirit of individual enterprise into public transport . . .".

To the committed entrepeneur passing the CPC (and possibly the PSV driving test as well) will be mere selection hurdles en route to becoming a profitable PSV franchisee. Neither should it be overlooked that although 40% of small businesses fail in the first three years of trading, a much higher proportion of those which succeed are franchises. If nothing else, the first operator to franchise out his or her minibus operations will have solved many problems of driver motivation!

Minibuses and taxis

Minibuses are known to generate traffic. Some but by no means all of this comes from competitors' services but much is composed of passengers who never would have used the existing bus services. In some cases, quite obviously, they would have used private cars and taxis.

In other cases the traffic is made up of passengers who simply would not have made the journey were it not for the new minibus service. There is some evidence, certainly with leisure and social traffic, that passengers may travel into town by minibus and return by taxi, despite the fact that many minibus services continue later into the night (often past "closing time") than the conventional bus service which they replaced.

Naturally taxi operators are apprehensive of new minibus schemes, fearing, in some cases with justification, a degree of abstraction from what they see as their traffic. However, the Transport Act 1985 has given taxi operators a degree of freedom which they too did not have before deregulation. And yet they are surprisingly reluctant to use this.

There is little evidence, outside London (where the scheme was implemented at Heathrow and mainline stations by the Department of Transport) of taxi operators asking their local licensing authority (District Council) to provide designated ranks from which they can carry passengers at separate fares. Nor is there much evidence of any wide use of such services or even of private hire cars being hired in advance at separate fares.

The provisions in the Transport Act 1985 which allow licensed taxi (but not private hire car) operators to obtain special restricted licences and register local services have been a damp squib. Attempts by one PTE to secure all night services on lightly used routes on this basis failed due to lack of interest by the local taxi trade. Only in rural areas have a few taxibus services emerged, supported by the Development Commission or the Scottish and Welsh Offices under their powers to make direct subsidies towards "innovative" improvements to rural services.

Taxi operators also feel betrayed by deregulation since the Act removes their own monopoly powers, in so far as local authorities can only refuse licences to new entrants to the taxi trade if they can demonstrate that there is "no significant unmet demand" in their area, a seemingly impossible task.

One of the favourite "honeypots" of taxis and private hire cars is out of town hypermarkets and shopping centres. These are often more accessible to minibuses than they were to conventional buses, and shrewd operators are already scheduling their services to call. The new bus station outside the renowned Metrocentre at Gateshead is packed with minibuses (and conventional buses) but the pointer to the future must surely be the Merryhill out-of-town shopping complex in the West Midlands which from the day it opened was served by a minibus network created for that very purpose.

School minibuses

A particular concern of schools and colleges is the liability which they incur as operators of minibuses. Since most of these are operated under the permit arrangements in the Transport Act 1985 which allow the non commercial use of the vehicle for hire and reward, the "school" becomes the operator of the vehicle.

The Public Passenger Vehicles Act 1981 says that the operator of a bus is the driver, if he or she is the owner, or the person for whom he or she drives whether under a contract of employment or any other form of contract personally to do the work.

In practice, both the driver, who will usually be a teacher, and the Headmaster, will have the same employer. Strictly this is the governing body of the school, college or even, where they run these, polytechnic or university but in practice it is the Local Education Authority or the DES.

However, the interpretation of employer in the context of bus operation is not conditional on the strict performance of a contract of employment, but rather depends upon whether the vehicle is driven on the employer's business and under his or her control. (This is analogous to the way in which, under the Health and Safety at Work, etc Act 1974 an employee manager can be construed as the employer of a subordinate). Thus a Head or Principal could be construed to be the operator responsible for the lawful use of the minibus.

Clearly the driver of the minibus may commit an offence such as speeding, overloading, or a traffic offence without the knowledge of the Head, or operator, in which case only the driver would be prosecuted as the user of the vehicle. However, the "operator" might be held to have caused the vehicle to be used illegally. For example by using his or her authority to give the driver an express or implied instruction, or to permit an illegal use in so far as he or she had knowledge of this but aquiesced to it. In this case the operator, as well as the driver, may be prosecuted for "causing" or "permitting" the offence. The operator's own licence could even be endorsed.

An extreme example might be where he or she prevails on a driver to make an "essential" trip, say to a sports fixture, knowing the vehicle to be unroadworthy. Undoubtedly he or she then causes the driver to commit an offence. In the same way, if he or she knows, or should have known that the vehicle is continually being used illegally by staff and does nothing to stop this, the operator has permitted the offence.

The operator can avoid this liability by drafting strict rules for the use of the minibus which not only forbid illegal practices but which require drivers to carry out essential checks of the bus and its equipment before each journey and report any defects occurring during its use.

One offence which can easily be committed with a school minibus is that of using it outside the conditions on the Permit. For example the Permit may have been issued by a designatory body such as the Boy Scouts' Association to the school scout troop and the bus may later have been used to transport the school basketball team.

Permits, as explained in Chapter 2, are made out for the carriage of a specific passenger class. In the case in question this could be, for example, Class A – members of the Permit issuing body, thus rendering the operation an illegal use of the permit by the scout troop, as operators.

However, since Permits are no longer "vehicle specific", if the school also had a Permit for a minibus issued by the Local Education Authority, it would be in order to borrow the Scouts' minibus provided the Permit disc issued by the LEA were transferred to it. In this case the Head would once again become the operator responsible for the condition and lawful use of that vehicle on the road.

The fact that Permits are not vehicle specific does, fortunately, make it easy for a school with a minibus Permit to hire in a minibus from a vehicle hire company, simply by displaying the Permit in the hire vehicle. It should be remembered that the school or operator is still responsible for the condition of that vehicle, even though the hire contract may include maintenance and repairs. This facility to hire in can be useful if the school minibus does not have a tachograph and it is decided to take students abroad using a hired vehicle with a tachograph.

When a minibus is used on an international journey, a tachograph must be fitted and used, and the drivers must observe EC drivers' hours regulations and keep a record of their hours of work and driving using a tachograph chart. Also a waybill and model control document (a copy of the waybill in the language of the countries which are party to ASOR – an international agreement on the carriage of passengers by road) must be carried, irrespective of whether the minibus is used for hire and reward, non-commercially or even as a private vehicle.

Operating an "occasional" service (as the EC defines one off school journey parties) without a waybill is an offence. Waybills and model control documents can be obtained from: Bus and Coach Council, Sardinia House, 52 Lincoln's Inn Fields, London WC2A 3LZ.

Although an insurance certificate issued by a Member State suffices as proof of third party cover within the EC, it is advisable to inform the insurer of the minibus that Continental cover is required. For a small additional premium to cover all comprehensive risks, the insurer will issue a "green card". This incorporates an accident report form on which agreed and non-contentious facts can be recorded and signed against by both parties after an accident. A green card is essential on Continental journeys to countries outside the EC.

On journeys to the Continent a minibus must be driven by a driver in possession of a full United Kingdom driving licence who is over 21 years of age. When the new European single driving licence, referred to in Chapter 3, becomes mandatory, it may be necessary for the driver to have a PCV (passenger carrying vehicle) licence for minibuses with 9–16 seats unless the United Kingdom succeeds in obtaining a derogation from Brussels.

It should be remembered that in the EC a minibus is a PCV. No distinction is made between PSVs and non PSVs.

The rural mini

In Chapter 1 it was pointed out that as long ago as 1961 the report by Professor Jack on Rural Bus Services had found that minibuses were "not the universal panacea". In Chapter 7 it is pointed out that the minibus is best used where demand is at "medium level", continuous and spontaneous. It is none of these things in rural areas.

Nonetheless, the minibus does have a place in rural transport. There are numerous small market towns of 5000 to 10,000 inhabitants which can support a town minibus service replacing an unsuccessful conventional bus service. The TRRL report on NBC minibus schemes lists 28 small towns with three or less minibuses operating in 1986, including, amongst others, in order of their introduction:

Barnstaple
Yeovil
Cirencester
Abingdon
Trowbridge
Nailsea
Melksham
Bideford
Wells
Kidsgrove
Ashby de la Zouch
Beverley.

One of the more exciting post deregulation developments in deep rural areas is the emergence of transport brokers on the staffs of "Shire" Counties' Transport Co-ordinators. The role of these officers is to encourage the provision of public transport in rural areas by helping to match supply and demand and by advising operators and providers such as Community Bus schemes, voluntary organisations like WVS car pools, and educational and social service departments how they might co-operate to solve each others' problems.

For example, in one Yorkshire Dale before a rationalisation scheme was devised, every morning and evening a tendered bus, a "sitting" ambulance, a postvan, a works bus and a school bus all ran up the valley with an average of less than three passengers each.

Reference has been made in Chapter 1 to the "Rutex" experiments, and the Transport Act 1985 now makes such rationalisations easier in two ways. First there is the duty of tendering authorities, Local Education Authorities and social services to co-operate so as to obtain the best value for money for their ratepayers in the provision of transport services and secondly, there is the fact that minibus Permits are no longer vehicle specific.

In other words, the school can "borrow" the Scouts' minibus and use it under their Permit. Transport brokers are succeeding in breaking down the natural reticence of minibus operators, where these are not PSV operators, to lending out their vehicles by pointing out the commercial sense of this where it can be done for reward, even if the price charged only covers the vehicle's marginal costs and makes some contribution to its overheads.

It could be that minibus pooling systems may succeed in providing an extremely basic level of rural service in some communities where there is not the commercial potential even for a Community Bus. In other rural areas where there is a modicum of traffic potential, of course, it has been shown that the Community Minibus (see Chapter 2) is a viable proposition.

Minibuses ten years on

Flavour of the month or brainwave of the decade? "Sic transit gloria mundi" or wall to wall minibuses in 2000 AD? Only time will tell. Much must depend on what social, economic, political and technological factors will be found ten years from now.

This book has rehearsed the arguments for the minibus. Certainly it has not been my intention to deny that some threats and doubts must hang over its future. What I hope I have done is to bring to a wider audience the case for the minibus in the hope that it will become even more widely appreciated and have a long and prosperous operational lifespan. If, in years to come, it must retire, I hope it can depart as gracefully as did the tram and trolleybus. Then, perhaps, in our children's time, like the tram, it may return.

APPENDIX *Traffic Areas*

Note: Correspondence should be addressed to the "Clerk to the Traffic Commissioner"–

Area and address

Scottish
83 Princes Street,
Edinburgh EH2 2ER.
Tel: 031–225 4979
Telex: 72614
Fax: 031–225 5494. Ext. 312

North Western
Portcullis House,
Seymour Grove,
Stretford,
Manchester M16 0NE.
Tel: 061–872 5077
Telex: 668849

North Eastern
Westgate House,
Westgate Road,
Newcastle upon Tyne
NE1 1TW.
Tel: 091–261 0031
Telex: 53351

Hillcrest House,
386 Harehills Lane,
Leeds LS9 6NF.
Tel: 0532 495661
Telex: 557427

Area covered

whole of Scotland

Cumbria, Lancashire,
Merseyside,
Greater Manchester,
Chesire, Clwyd, Gwynnedd,
Borough of High Peak (in
Derbyshire).

Northumberland,
Tyne and Wear,
Durham, Cleveland,
Part of North Yorkshire (covering
Northallerton, Catterick and
Richmond areas).

North Yorkshire (except the part
dealt with by the Newcastle
office),
West Yorkshire, South Yorkshire,
Humberside.

106

West Midland

Cumberland House,
200 Broad Street,
Birmingham B15 1TD
Tel: 021-631 3300
Telex: 338841

Staffordshire,
Shropshire,
West Midlands,
Warwickshire,
Hereford and Worcester.

Eastern

Terrington House,
13–15 Hills Road,
Cambridge CB2 1NP.
Tel: 0223 358922
Telex: 81373

Bedfordshire, Cambridgeshire,
Norfolk, Suffolk,
Essex (except the District of
Basildon, Brentwood, Epping
Forest and Harlow and
Borough of Thurrock).

Birkbeck House,
14–16 Trinity Square,
Nottingham NG1 4BA.
Tel: 0602 475511
Telex: 37188

Derbyshire (except Borough
of High Peak),
Nottinghamshire, Lincolnshire,
Leicester, Northamptonshire.

South Wales

Caradog House,
1–6 St Andrews Place,
Cardiff CF1 3PW.
Tel: 0222 394238
Telex: 497011/SWALTRAF
   CARDIFF
Fax: 0222 371675

Powys, Dyfed,
West Glamorgan, Mid Glamorgan,
South Glamorgan, Gwent.

Western

The Gaunt's House,
Denmark Street,
Bristol BS1 5DR.
Tel: 0272 297221
Telex: 44647

Gloucestershire, Avon,
Wiltshire, Somerset, Dorset,
Devon, Cornwall.

Metropolitan

PO Box 643
Charles House,
375 Kensington High Street,
London W14 8QU
Tel: 01-605 0365
Telex: 28639-METRAF
Fax: 01-605 0499
GTN No 2570

All London boroughs,
Hertfordshire,
Surrey (except the Borough of
Surrey Heath and the District
of Waverley),
The Districts of Basildon, Brentwood,
Epping Forest and Harlow
and the Borough of Thurrock
(in Essex),
The Borough of Dartford and the
District of Sevenoaks (in Kent).

South Eastern

Ivy House,
3 Ivy Terrace,
Eastbourne BN21 4QT.
Tel: 0323 21471
Telex: 87335

Buckinghamshire, Oxfordshire,
Berkshire, Hampshire,
Isle of Wight, West Sussex,
East Sussex, Kent (except the
Borough of Dartford
and the District of Sevenoaks),
Borough of Surrey Heath and District
of Waverley (in Surrey).

Index